The Russian Artist

RUSSIA OLD AND NEW SERIES
Jules Koslow, General Editor

The Russian Artist
THE CREATIVE PERSON IN RUSSIAN CULTURE

Tobia Frankel

The Macmillan Company, New York, New York
Collier-Macmillan Ltd., London

The Macmillan Company
866 Third Avenue, New York, N.Y. 10022
Collier-Macmillan Canada Ltd., Toronto,
Ontario

Library of Congress Catalog Card Number:
72–78617

First Printing

Printed in the United States of America

Gratefully, to my family

Contents

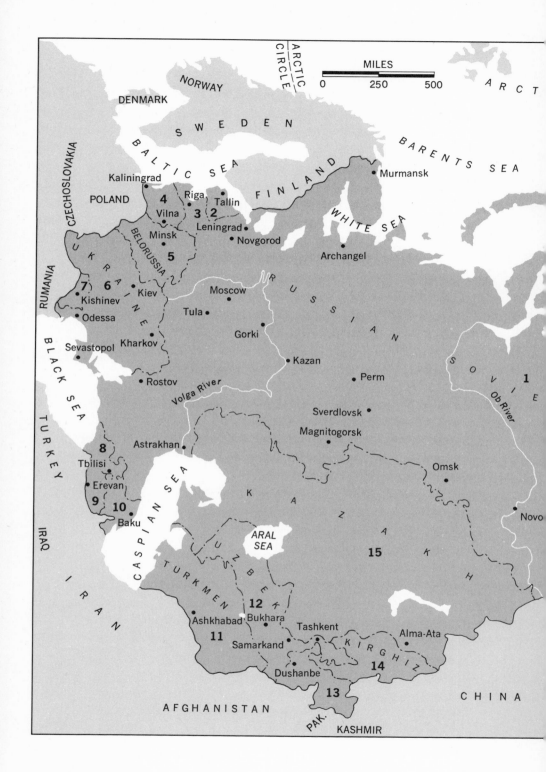

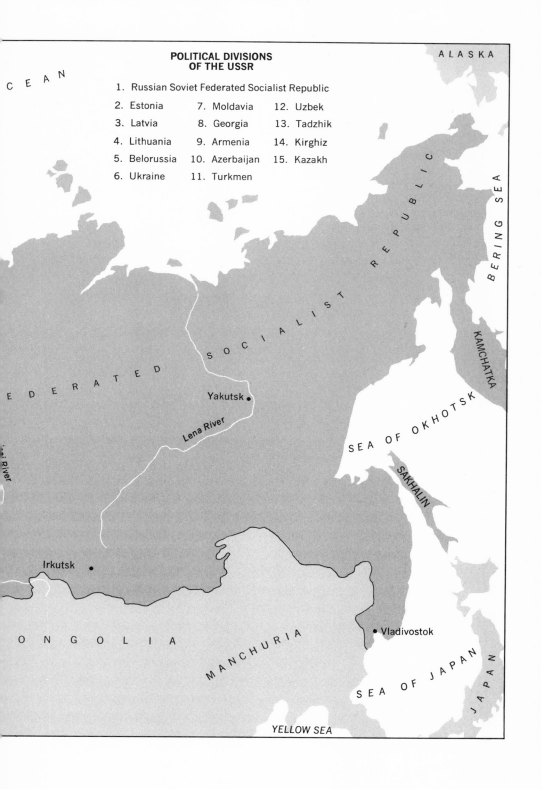

**POLITICAL DIVISIONS
OF THE USSR**

1. Russian Soviet Federated Socialist Republic

2. Estonia   7. Moldavia   12. Uzbek

3. Latvia   8. Georgia   13. Tadzhik

4. Lithuania   9. Armenia   14. Kirghiz

5. Belorussia   10. Azerbaijan   15. Kazakh

6. Ukraine   11. Turkmen

Introduction:
A Tale of Three Cities

A SOVIET writer was expelled from Moscow University a few years ago because he wrote a paper about the Norman influence on early Russian civilization. "The official ideology," the writer explained, "is that Russian history was not influenced by any other culture."[1]

Although some Soviet Russians find it difficult to concede their debt to other cultures, Western historians believe that Christianity —imported from Byzantium in 988—brought to the Kievan Russians an alphabet, a literature, an art, an architecture, and an orientation to the Western world that still confuses Russian rulers and arouses in them the conflicting desires to imitate and to denounce it.

From the fifteenth to the eighteenth centuries, the czars borrowed eagerly from the West: Italians constructed the Kremlin churches; Germans established the first dramatic theater in the czar's court; French writers charmed the nobility. In the nineteenth century, hav-

1. *New York Times*, Dec. 24, 1967.

1

ing assimilated and digested these Western influences, Russian writers, poets, painters, and musicians produced a national culture that
continues to give pleasure to audiences at home and abroad. And, in
the early years of this century, as if to pay a debt of centuries, Russian painters such as Kandinsky and Malevich created new artistic
forms and philosophical perspectives for the entire Western world;
the composers Stravinsky and Prokofiev amazed Paris and New York
with their innovations in modern music; and Diaghilev's Ballet Russe
starring Karsavina, Pavlova, and Nijinsky, astonished European audiences with its perfection of a Western art. Stanislavsky's studio
method was to become the inspiration of actors everywhere and
especially in the American theater. But by the middle of the twentieth century—with communication technically easier than ever before—the Soviet rulers tried to shun cultural relations with the West.
In the ideological battle between capitalism and communism, between democracy and totalitarianism, they put blinders on their nation to avoid all distraction from the course they decreed for it.

This forced estrangement from the West is significant because it
denies artists contact with the ideas of their colleagues abroad. It
also denied the West contact with Russian culture just at the moment when it had achieved worldwide acclaim.

Today the Soviet Union spreads across the continents of Europe
and Asia, occupying one-sixth of the world's surface, and containing
more than 240 million people. Three cities dominate its history: the
country was born a thousand years ago in the pagan city-state of
Kiev; its adolescent years were dominated by the dukedom of
Muscovy; and the growing pains of youth were induced by Peter the
Great from his capital, St. Petersburg. It came of age as a twentieth-
century world power, with the government based again in the medieval capital of Moscow. The three great cities of Russia—Kiev, Moscow, St. Petersburg—achieved their eminence because they offered
an indispensable feature: water. In the ninth century, the area that
later became known as Russia was just a series of disconnected city-
states. Kiev's distinction among them was that it lay at the southern
end of the north-south water road, starting at the Baltic Sea and
winding along the Volkhov River past Novgorod, the northern end
of the road; along the Lovat and Dvina rivers, at Smolensk, the mid-
point, and finally reaching Kiev on the Dnieper. Below Kiev the

Dnieper flows to the Black Sea and thence to Constantinople, where the early Slavic tribes traded their furs, wax, honey, and slaves. This was the route traveled by the Vikings from Scandinavia, whose leader Rurik became the prince of Novgorod, and whose countryman, Oleg, conquered Kiev in 882 and set about uniting the cities into a nation. In the fourteenth century, the center of power shifted to Moscow, north and east of Kiev, astride another trading route. This second lifeline ran northwest to southeast along the Volga and Oka rivers, flowing into the Caspian Sea. Both these water routes, however, still trapped Russia inside the Asian land mass and her rulers soon came to long for outlets to the rest of Europe in the West, whence came their ideas of civilization, learning, and technology.

Under Ivan the Terrible in the sixteenth century, the Russians began to stretch toward a northern all-weather outlet on the Baltic Sea. A century later Peter the Great realized the dream, defeating the Swedes who held the territory he needed, and establishing his new capital, St. Petersburg, in 1713. Ever since then St. Petersburg has been Russia's "window on the West." The story of these three capitals is the story not only of Russia's history but also of her culture. As presented here, the evolution of Russian art and artists—writers, musicians, painters, architects, dancers—is traced through the history of Kiev, Moscow, and St. Petersburg, and then back again to Moscow, after the Communist Revolution of 1917.

The revolution altered not only Russia's name—in 1922 it officially became the Union of Soviet Socialist Republics—but also the entire social structure, including the relationship between the artist and the state. It is therefore convenient and customary to refer to the pre-revolutionary period as Russian and the post-revolutionary epoch as Soviet.

1. Kiev: A Southern Exposure (882-1240)

RUSSIAN cultural history begins with Kiev, the first capital of the future Russian empire, because that is where Christianity and therefore Western culture first came to Russia. And it is from Kiev that literature, music, architecture, and art were first disseminated. Kiev is where hundreds of craftsmen toiled anonymously to duplicate the art of Byzantium. And Kiev is where the first Russian dynasty was established, which ruled from 882 to 1613.

In most of western Europe in medieval times, religion was not only a spiritual outlet and a philosophic explanation of the universe; it also provided the framework for all knowledge and culture. The efforts to spread Christian doctrine led to the construction of awe-inspiring structures: churches with sky-scratching steeples, frescoed walls, and colorful stained glass windows. Musical pageantry was created for these churches and biblical law and lore were passed down in written as well as oral forms. Religion, as the source of man's knowledge, molded his culture. Inspired by religion, man's art had only religious functions.

To recruit Slav adherents to the faith two Greek missionaries, Cyril

Comparative chart of Greek
and Cyrillic alphabets.

GREEK	CYRILLIC
A	а
Б	Б(v) Б(b)
<Λ	г
DΔⵁ	д
ϝ	є
ϙ F	ж
H	н(i)
I	I(i)
к	к
ſ	л
M	M
ʌ	н
ⵁ ⟡	о
г	п
Ϙ	
Р	ф
⟨	с
T	T
V	
X	х (h)
	у (u)
エ	ж(ʒ)ѕ(ѕ)з
Ŧ +	

and Methodius, developed in Bulgaria in 863 an alphabet based on
Greek characters. Later known as Cyrillic after one of the monks,
this alphabet was adopted by the Slavic tribes of southeastern Europe. By mixing Slavic dialect with a Greek structure the monks also
created a formal language used mainly in religious and literary pur-
suits. Known as Church Slavonic, it differed markedly from the
vernacular or spoken language of the Slavs.

For what was probably a combination of political and aesthetic
reasons, Vladimir, the grand duke of Kiev, preferred the Greek Orthodox version of Christianity, then centered in Constantinople, over
the Western Catholic version, centered in Rome. Vladimir made his
choice of faith after sending envoys to Bulgaria, Germany, and
Greece. Their report shows they were impressed by only one place:
"When we journeyed among the Bulgarians we beheld how they
worship in their temple, called a mosque, while they stand ungirt.
The Bulgarian bows, sits down, looks hither and thither like one pos-
sessed, and there is no happiness among them, but instead only sor-

row and a dreadful stench. Their religion is not good. Then we went among the Germans, and saw them performing many ceremonies in their temples; but we beheld no glory there. Then we went on to Greece, and the Greeks led us to the edifices where they worship their God, and we knew not whether we were in heaven or on earth. For on earth there is no such splendor or such beauty. . . ."[1]

Thus, the harmonious beauty of the Eastern church service, its music, ornate costumes, wall paintings, and sweet-smelling incense appealed to the Russians, and they transported the artifacts and elements of the church to the north.

An immediate consequence of Vladimir's conversion, in 988, was the destruction of all aspects of pagan worship among the early Russians. Primitive temples and totem-pole idols to the gods of nature —Perun, god of thunder; Dazhdbog, god of sun; Stribog, god of wind; Veles, god of cattle; Mokosh, goddess of water—were replaced with churches. Though some Christian churches had existed in Kiev for more than a hundred years—from the time of Vladimir's grandmother—they were small, wooden structures and not central to the life of the city.

Now, with the need to accommodate many more people and a desire to celebrate his conversion with something grandiose, Vladimir planned a stone cathedral, to match the impressive St. Sophia in Constantinople. The new structure required skilled craftsmen and Vladimir sent for Greek architects and builders to construct his Church of the Assumption.

This was the first of many calls for Western craftsmen and advisers by Russian leaders over the centuries. The Greeks who moved to Kiev were the precursors of Italians who journeyed to Moscow to build the Kremlin, of Germans who established the Russian theater, of the Dutch in St. Petersburg who helped Peter the Great build ships, of the French encyclopedists who advised Catherine the Great on her art purchases and collections.

But this pattern of borrowing should not becloud two aspects of Russian artistic development. Even in the tenth century, the native Russians were skilled craftsmen who worked well in wood and other

---

1. Serge A. Zenkovsky, *Medieval Russia's Epics, Chronicles and Tales* (New York: E. P. Dutton, 1963), p. 67.

materials; their embroidery, pottery and jewelry designs showed traces of the influence of the Scythians, who had roamed the same plains as long ago as the fifth century B.C. Secondly, the Russians' admiration for Byzantine culture did not prevent them from shrewdly adapting it to their own needs and endowing it with peculiarly Russian characteristics.

This was particularly noticeable in architecture, the art form in which the early Russians displayed great originality. Although the first stone church built by Vladimir followed the Byzantine pattern of a cross—with three apses and a dome roof resting on piers—two other Russian cathedrals built in Kiev and Novgorod within fifty years inaugurated a new style. The Russians emphasized the church dome, putting it higher than the Byzantine original and surrounding it with twelve smaller domes, representing the twelve apostles, to create an exciting cluster.

Eventually, the low flat dome of Byzantium was transformed by Russian hands into a tall bulb, shaped like an onion, and colorfully painted, gilded, or shingled in wood. This bulbous shape was not only distinctive architecturally, but also physically practical; snow rolled off the new church roofs much more easily than off the old.

When Vladimir's sons moved north and northeast after his death, each assuming control of different parts of his domain, similar churches and palaces had to be built in Novgorod, Vladimir, and Suzdal. The northern churches were boxier than the Byzantine, appearing more vertical than horizontal. Their height, white exteriors, and ornamental, sculptured facades made them more impressive on the flat Russian landscape. Laborers building them carted white limestone day and night from the quarries of the lower Oka valley to the hill of Vladimir.

Within a half century of Vladimir's conversion Kiev acquired more than four hundred new churches, and a great many people were employed in their construction and maintenance. Many of the craftsmen came from the new clergy; others were attached to the royal household. Foreign craftsmen were also drawn from the Caucasus in the south and from as far away as Rome.

Church records make only a few references to the craftsmen employed in book illustrating, church building, icon and fresco painting, cloisonné enameling, and embossed metalwork. But a few names

The low flat dome of Byzantium, as seen in Hagia Sophia in Constantinople (*above*), was transformed in Russia into a tall, onion-shaped bulb. *The Bettmann Archive and Sovfoto*

have filtered down through the ages, including those of the eleventh-century carpenter Mironeg, the builder Jdan Nikola, and the painter-monk Alimpi of the Monastery of the Caves in Kiev.

Throughout the two hundred and fifty years of Kiev's preeminence, before it was overrun in 1240 by Asiatic hordes, icon painting was generally left to the Byzantine masters. The icons—religious paintings on wood—were characterized by heavily stylized draping of garments, solemn expressions on the faces of the saints, and by generally dark colors and a strict limitation of subject matter. The Virgin, Trinity scenes from the Old and New Testaments, and saints were the favored themes.

Russian church music, too, adhered to the Byzantine tradition of monodic chant which lacked the counterpoint and harmonies that later developed in the music of the Roman church. Sculpture was not allowed in the churches in obedience to the biblical commandment forbidding the making of graven images.

The early Russian literature also lacked native characteristics. Monks and priests composed the written records that have survived, using the Church Slavonic language. This "literature" was limited to copies of the Bible, religious tracts, histories of saints, and factual chronicles that made no evaluation of the events they described. By contrast, the oral "literature" of ordinary people was much richer, consisting of folk songs, fairy tales, proverbs and *byliny*—epic poems or chants that recounted the glories of knights and wars in vibrant images, rhymes, and rhythms.

The byliny, "that which has been," were passed from generation to generation by *skazitels,* or storytellers, but their authors are unknown. Most were not even written down until the eighteenth and nineteenth centuries.

The only one known to have been composed and written down in medieval times is *The Word of the Campaign of Igor,* a stirring account of the battles of Prince Igor from Novgorod-Seversk against the Kumans, a nomadic, warlike tribe of southern Russia. The battle occurred in 1185 and it is assumed that the anonymous author wrote the epic ballad soon after. In 1795 a sixteenth-century version of it was discovered in a monastery by a famous Russian collector, Count Mussin-Pushkin. He published the poem in 1800; this was fortunate because the manuscript and a copy he had made perished when Napoleon set Moscow on fire in 1812.

The description of the battles between Igor's armies and the Kumans, his capture and escape, and the impassioned lamentations of his wife are filled with simple, naturalistic images:

> Igor looked up at the bright sun,
> And saw that all his warriors
> became enveloped in darkness.
> And Igor spoke to his army:
>   "Brethren and Warriors!
>   It is better to be killed in battle
>   than to become a captive.
>   Let us mount our swift steeds, brethren!
>   Let us view the blue river Don."

> And the prince's mind was seized by ambition.
> And the desire to drink from the great river Don
> concealed the evil omens from him.
> And he spoke:
>   "I want to break a lance at the Kuman frontier.
>   I want, oh, my Russians,
>   either to drink with you Don [water] from my helmet,
>   or to leave my head there."[2]

Although it was written two hundred years after the Russians' conversion to Christianity, there are still references to the pagan gods in *The Word*. There are also references to an earlier balladeer, Boyan the Seer, "grandson of God Veles," an eleventh-century bard who was "the nightingale of yore":

> For he, Boyan the Seer,
> When composing a song to someone
> soared in his thoughts over the tree [of wisdom],
> ran as a gray wolf over the land,
> flew below the clouds as a blue-gray eagle . . .

2. *Ibid.*, pp. 140–141.

and

> . . . he lay his wise fingers
> Upon the living strings
> and they sounded lauds to the princes.

And this is how the author recounts the sorrow of Igor's wife, Euphrosinia Yaroslavna:

> At the river Danube lances sing their song,
> but it is the voice of Yaroslavna which is heard.
> Since morning, she sings like an unknown seagull:
>   "Like a seagull I will fly along the river Danube.
>   I will dip my beaver-trimmed sleeve into the river Kaiala.
>   I will cleanse the bloody wounds of my prince,
>   on his mighty body."

Since morning Euphrosinia has lamented on the walls of the city of Putivl, saying:

> "O wind, why do you, my lord wind,
>   blow so fiercely?
> Why do you bring on your light wings
> Kuman arrows against the warriors of my beloved?
> Isn't it enough for you to blow under the clouds,
> to loll the ships on the blue sea?
> Why, my lord, did you scatter my joy
> over the feather grass of the prairie?"[3]

The Word is unique not only for its lyrical beauty and vivid imagery, but also because it united the oral epic tradition with the written language of Church Slavonic.

Because of the multinational character of the Byzantine empire at the time that it adopted Christianity, the church made no effort to impose the Greek language on its imperial possessions. Contrary to the policies of Rome, Byzantium allowed each national group within the empire to translate the Bible and the religious service into its own

3. *Ibid.*, pp. 139, 140, 156–157.

language. Thus from the time of Vladimir's conversion, the Russian church service and all religious books were translated into Church Slavonic. This offered certain advantages to the Russian monks and bookmen, but it also kept them from learning Greek and encountering the humanist tradition of the Greek classics. It prolonged their isolation from important currents of Western thought and Kiev's capture by the Tatars in 1240 cut them off even longer.

The scepter of leadership fell from Kiev primarily because of quarrels over who should hold it, leaving the city defenseless against the Mongolian Tatars from the east. For the next hundred years, while the dukes of Moscow were moving to fill the vacuum by purchasing and seizing land, the princes and merchants of Novgorod in the north were left as the preeminent bearers of Russian culture.

It was a Novgorod prince, Alexander Nevsky, who dealt with the Tatars and became the first Russian prince to collect tribute for the conquerors. His city, situated at the northern end of the important north-south water road, traded with the south and the west and even joined the German Hanseatic League of European ports.

Although they controlled vast territories to the north, the Novgorodians were preoccupied with money and commerce, not with the creation of a political state centered in their city. With their wealth, however, they were able to support many artists and the building of many churches. The Novgorod school of architecture made unique contributions to the Russian artistic heritage; its primarily wooden churches sprouted cone-shaped roofs topped by a single bulb, and its icons, more naturalistic than the severe stylistic paintings of Byzantium, showed a Western influence and—to the dismay of the church—had a subversive impact on Muscovite painters.

But it was the dukes of Moscow who conclusively defeated the Tatars in 1480. Eight years later they formally absorbed Novgorod by starving it into submission.

2. Moscow: Triumph over the East (1340-1713)

MUSCOVY, or Moscow, had now grown a hundredfold into a sizeable territory, the equal of many European countries. Her dukes began to call themselves czars (that is, Caesars) and autocrats (meaning first, independent, and then dominant, rulers). They induced peasants to settle the newly acquired territories and gradually bound them to the land.

In 1533 Ivan IV, later dubbed the Terrible, had himself crowned czar; he was the first Moscow ruler to do so. But he and his successors still shared power with the Byzantine church. In fact, when Ivan's descendants and their rivals fell into what is called the "time of troubles," trying to decide who belonged on the throne, it was the church that helped to hold the realm together.

The political system was not stabilized again until the throne fell to the Romanov family in 1613. Now a succession of czars consolidated the power of the throne while jurisdictional conflicts and arguments over liturgical reform bitterly divided the church. When Peter the Great became czar in 1682, he left vacant the patriarchate, the highest church office, while aggressively undermining both its political and cultural influence.

14

Architecture and then art in this Moscow period became essentially Russian in character. As long as the church retained equal power, the realm's music and literature remained essentially religious, and derivative from the Byzantine. But the church's decline in the seventeenth century brought not only a new secularism but also a new infusion of Western ideas. Probably the crucial cultural event of the period was Moscow's reunion in 1667 with Kiev—not the old Kiev, but a region transformed by several hundred years of association with Lithuania and Poland and their Roman Catholic religion. The expansion in the south brought not merely more territory but entirely new forms of art and music as well as a continuing point of contact with Western Europe.

Russian culture was to be deeply affected by the events of the sixteenth and seventeenth centuries. The peasants that were being bound to the land by a system of serfdom would eventually become the musicians, actors, and dancers of Russia, the bearers of her art. The dramatic conflicts of the "time of troubles" and the forceful personalities and policies of Ivan and Peter were to provide raw material for Russian artists for centuries to come. And the confrontation with Western ideas and styles posed sharp questions of the relative merits of native and alien cultures, questions that have tormented Russia ever since.

In Moscow, as in early Kiev, religious architecture flourished. And it was now joined by an evolving national school of icon painting. The great Russian innovation of the fourteenth century merged construction and painting to produce the iconostasis, a wall covered with icons that separated the main hall of the church from its holy sanctuary.

The wooden icons were hung as sacred objects not only in churches but also in private homes, usually in a corner of the main room. They often depicted saints, the intermediaries between God and his people. Whenever an icon failed to fulfill the prayers of a pleader, it was "punished" by being turned to the wall. To protect the icons from dust, the people covered them with screens; in wealthier homes, they were encased in silver—often so elaborately that only the saint's face remained visible. Because of their religious and artistic attributes, icons were highly valued and bequeathed from one generation to the next.

The icons were created by Russian monks and Greek painters, several of whom are known by name. They did not sign their works, but biographical information gleaned from church records identifies different artists with different churches at particular times.

Thus it is known that Theophanes the Greek (circa 1335–1410) worked in Novgorod for twenty-five years until 1395, and thereafter in Moscow. He refused to be bound by the manuals and conventions of Byzantine art, which strictly prescribed subject matter, color, and form, but insisted on his own style. It was distinguishable by short, impressionistic strokes of the brush, elongation of figures, subdued use of color, and portrayal of heads in three-quarter view rather than fullface. His work had a great influence on Russian icon painters, particularly on Andrei Rublev.

Andrei Rublev (circa 1360–1430), a monk attached to the Monastery of the Trinity-Sergius, is first mentioned as working with Theophanes on an iconostasis for a Moscow cathedral. He is regarded as Russia's greatest native icon painter, even by the modern Soviet government which established a Rublev Museum on the six-hundredth anniversary of his birth.

The Trinity, an icon by Andrei Rublev. *Sovfoto*

Following Theophanes' lead, Rublev also broke with the accepted aesthetic conventions. His harmonious natural colors, delicate lines, and serene moods reveal the depth of his faith and a keen power of observation. One Soviet critic, in fact, has found in Rublev's colors not only religious faith but the artist's native Russian landscape: "His marvelous deep blue is suggested by the blue of the spring sky; his whites recall the birches so dear to a Russian; his green is close to the color of unripe rye; his golden ochre summons up memories of fallen autumn leaves; in his dark green colors there is something of the twilight shadows of the dense pine forest. . . ."[1]

The first layman who became a religious painter and ran a professional workshop was Dionysius (circa 1440–1505), who lived a hundred years after Rublev. More and more the icon painters had to be drawn from the common people. They were in great demand to meet the fast pace of building in the capital—a pace due in part to the frequent fires and earthquakes that destroyed the wooden churches and their decorations. Calls for painters often went from Moscow to Novgorod, and those who refused to respond often were brought forcibly.

The corps of native painters was augmented at the end of the fifteenth century by numerous Italian architects who were brought to Russia at the suggestion of Sophie, the second wife of Ivan III. The niece of the last Byzantine emperor, she had been raised in Rome and knew of the superior construction skills of the Italian workmen.

There was little doubt that these skills were needed. In 1472, the year of Ivan's marriage to Sophie, the walls of Moscow's Church of the Assumption collapsed in an earthquake for which its Russian architects had not prepared.

Three years later, the first Italian recruit arrived in Moscow. He was Ridolfo Fieravanti Aristotele, a sixty-year-old architect, engineer, and expert in hydraulics and military fortifications. He was paid ten rubles a month, then the equivalent of two silver pounds. He was followed throughout the rest of the century by technicians that Ivan summoned from Italy, among them Pietro Antonio Solario and Marco Ruffo.

---

1. Robert Wallace, *Rise of Russia* (New York: Time, Inc., 1967), p. 142.

The Italians worked in the Moscow Kremlin. Though known today as the supreme seat of power in Soviet Russia, the Moscow fortress was then just one of many in medieval Russia. It was a compound of palaces and churches, to which office buildings and theaters were added in more recent times. The Italian style is visible in its red brick wall, which replaced the earlier stone, and in the circular, strongly fortified towers at the corners of the wall. Inside the Kremlin walls, however, the Italians applied their engineering skills to Russian designs. They rebuilt the shaken Church of the Assumption, copying a masterpiece that Russians had erected three centuries earlier in Vladimir. The job was not without its hazards. Solario died after two years in Moscow, presumably from a cold contracted during construction of an underground water reservoir in one of the Kremlin's corner towers.

But the wide respect for foreigners undermined the morale of the Russian artisans. In the 1600s, a famous native iconographer, Simon Ushakov, was earning only 67 rubles a year after thirty years in the czar's service, while Antz Detters, a foreigner, received 250.

Though discriminated against, the Russian architects still received important assignments, one of the most famous being the Cathedral of St. Basil the Blessed, beside the Kremlin in Moscow's Red Square. Built by the architects Posnik and Barma Yakovlev of Pskov between 1555 and 1560, it features eight bulbous cupolas surrounding a central tent-roof. The profusion of color of the many sculptured surfaces and the intricacy of design create a bizarre and exciting effect.

A nineteenth-century French traveler, the Marquis de Custine, described the church as "a masterpiece of caprice," adding that "certainly the land where such a monument is called a place of prayer is not Europe; it is India, Persia, China, and the men who go to worship God in this box of glazed fruits are not Christians!"[2]

Despite Custine's scorn, Russians still tell an apocryphal story about how Ivan the Terrible ordered the architects blinded so that they could never again build anything so beautiful.

His reputation and appellation as "the Terrible" notwithstanding, Ivan IV was a vigorous patron of the arts. Like his grandfather, he

2. Astolphe Louis Léonard Custine, *Journey for Our Time. The Russian Journals of the Marquis de Custine,* trans. and ed. Phyllis Penn Kohler (New York: Pellegrini and Cudahy, 1951), p. 266.

The Cathedral of St. Basil the Blessed in Moscow's Red Square. *Sovfoto*

summoned West European craftsmen and also Russian icon painters, jewelers, filigree workers, enamelers, and goldsmiths from outside Moscow to the capital. In his Kremlin workshop he supervised
the production of icons, icon encasements, church vestments and
vessels. The erratically pious czar then presented them to churches
and monasteries throughout the land.

A sixteenth-century Englishman, Richard Chancellor, summarized
the luxury and beauty of the court after attending one of Ivan's banquets. He found the emperor "sitting upon a high and stately seat,
apparelled with a robe of silver, and with another diadem on his
head." On a table in front of the czar "was placed the emperor's plate,
which was so much that the very cupboard itself was scant able to
sustain the weight of it. The better part of all the vessels and goblets
were made of very fine gold. . . ."[3]

Ivan's interests were not limited to the plastic and decorative arts.
The first Russian printing press went into operation during his reign,
although not with the happiest of consequences. Soon after, the chief
printer, Ivan Fedorov, and his associate, Peter Mstislavits, had to
flee for their lives to Lithuania when their version of *The Apostles*
affronted ignorant clergymen and was burned by them.

Ivan also contributed to the religious and political theory of his
day. In a fascinating correspondence with one of his subjects, Prince
Andrei Kurbsky, he asserted the principle of the divine right of
kings: as czar he deemed himself God's agent on earth. His theories
justified the autocracy that was to rule Russia for three hundred and
fifty years.

His importation of foreign craftsmen had the unexpected effect of
undermining the influence of the Orthodox church whose sanctuaries
they had come to build and decorate. The Italians had adapted to
Russian styling and design, but other Western influences, passing
through Novgorod, were deemed subversive by the churchmen. In
particular they frowned on the more vibrant colors and more humanistic poses of figures in the Novgorod icons. Through their trade with
Western Europe, the Novgorodians came in contact with a naturalistic, pictorial art. In France, Italy, and Germany, art was no longer

3. Arthur Voyce, *The Moscow Kremlin* (Berkeley and Los Angeles: University of
California Press, 1954), p. 50.

restricted to religious motifs but had begun to emphasize man and his life.

The problems caused by such influences on icon painters were raised at a church council in 1551. Icon painters were ordered to "reproduce the ancient models, those of the Greek icon painters, of Andrei Rublev and other famous painters. . . . In nothing will the painters follow their own fancy."[4] The council even published a manual describing the established patterns in subject matter and form.

Despite these injunctions, the problem persisted. Instead of idealizing the religious figures, the artists humanized them. According to the priest Avvakum, they painted the "image of the Saviour Emmanuel with bloated face, red lips, swollen fingers, and large, fat legs and thighs. His whole figure that of a German, fat-bellied and corpulent. . . ."[5]

The patriarch Nikon, trying to halt the trend away from traditional Byzantine art, even ordered non-conforming icons burned, declaring them to have been "imported by Germans from the German land." The resentment of foreign influences that challenged official orthodoxy was to be a typical reaction of Russia's rulers throughout the nineteenth and twentieth centuries.

The painters defended their new style. Joseph Vladimirov wrote to his colleague Simon Ushakov, "Where and who found the instruction about painting the faces of the saints in dark, swarthy shades? Was the countenance of all mankind created alike? Were all the saints dark and gaunt? . . . Who among reasonable people would not laugh at the folly that prefers darkness and gloom to light? No, this is not the idea of a wise artist. . . . And as in the Old Testament so in the New have many saints, both male and female, appeared comely."[6] He also denied that beautiful icons could lead man to temptation, asserting that naturalism, not stylization, was the key to religious inspiration.

Actually, the swarthiness of face to which Vladimirov referred was often caused by the oils with which the icons were preserved.

4. George Heard Hamilton, *The Art and Architecture of Russia* (Harmondsworth, Middlesex, England: Penguin Books Ltd., 1954), p. 151.
5. Paul Miliukov, *Outlines of Russian Culture,* vol. III, ed. Michael Karpovich (Philadelphia: University of Pennsylvania Press, 1948), p. 43.
6. *Ibid.,* p. 44.

Over the centuries the darkened images thus produced came to be regarded as the original, essential iconographic rendering and therefore not to be altered.

The same kind of misconception—reverence for an acquired rather than inherent quality—led to the great religious schism of the seventeeth-century Russian church.

In 1654 a church assembly decreed the correction of mistranslations and misspellings in the Bible, demanding, for instance, that the name of Jesus be written Iisus instead of Isus. It ordered blessings given with three fingers upraised instead of two, as had become customary. Though the reforms were ordered to revive the practices of the mother church, some Russian congregations regarded the customs they had followed for centuries as doctrinally sound and superior and they rebelled against the reform. Those who resisted reform were thereafter known as the Old Believers, or *raskolniki* (dissenters). They were dogmatic in their devotion to the old traditions and often preferred exile to change.

Religion, which had dominated the graphic arts, continued to determine literary fashion as well. Sermons, religious essays, chronicles, and straightforward accounts of battles and events were cast in the traditional forms. Some secular tales drawn from everyday life appeared in the sixteenth and seventeeth centuries, but fiction in the modern sense did not develop until the nineteenth century.

An interesting example of the standard chronicle is provided by the fifteenth-century manuscript of a certain Afanasy Nikitin, a merchant of Tver. Entitled *Voyage Across Three Seas,* it is the account of that Russian Marco Polo's journey from Russia to India, and it appears to be typical of the secular writing style of the time:

Through the prayers of our Holy Fathers, O Lord Jesus Christ, Son of God, have mercy upon me, Thy sinful servant Afanasy, son of Nikita. I have described my sinful voyage beyond three seas, the first being the Sea of Derbent, or Sea of Khwalis [Caspian], the second the Indian Sea, or Sea of Hindustan, and the third the Black Sea, or Sea of Stambul. I set forth down the Volga from the Golden Domed Cathedral of the Redeemer, from Grand Duke Mikhail Borisovich and from his Grace Gennady of Tver. Upon arrival at Kalyazin, I received the blessing of Father-Superior Macarius and brethren of the Monastery of the Holy

Trinity and the Holy Martyrs Boris and Gleb; from Kalyazin I proceeded to Uglich, and from Uglich to Kostroma, to Prince Alexander,
bearing another pass from the Grand Duke, and he let me sail on un-
hampered. Nor was I hampered on my way to the city of Nizhny Novgorod, to Mikhail Kiselev, the Governor, and Ivan Sarayev, Keeper of the
Tolls.

Vasily Papin had already passed on, and for a fortnight I had to
wait at Novgorod the arrival of Hasan Beg, the Tartar Shirvanshah's
Ambassador. He was coming from Grand Duke Ivan with gerfalcons,
of which he had ninety. And I proceeded with him down the Volga.
We sailed freely past Kazan, the Horde, Uslan, Sarai, and Berekezan. . . .

In India strangers put up at inns, and the food is cooked for them by
women, who also make the guests' beds. In winter people there wear a
dhoti around their loins, another about their shoulders, and a third
around their heads. . . . The Indians eat no flesh at all—no beef, mutton,
fowl, fish, or pork, although they have a great many pigs. They have
two meals a day, and eat nothing at night; they drink neither wine nor
mead. . . . And they pray facing eastwards, in the Russian manner; they
raise high both hands and put them on their crown, and lie face
downwards on the ground and stretch out on it—that is how they worship. . . .[7]

Printing came to Russia in 1564, more than a century after Guten-
berg issued his first Bible in Germany. Even then it was not used
widely and two centuries later there were still more handwritten
manuscripts than books in Russia. But the press had an unusual effect
on the religious schism of the seventeenth century. The first presses
belonged to the church, which used them to reproduce copies of the
Bible and thus spread widely the very inaccuracies that it tried so
desperately later to correct.

Among the rebels against the new liturgical procedures was the
priest Avvakum (1621–1682). In punishment for his views, he was
deported to Siberia in 1653. He returned to Moscow nine years later,
still in opposition, and was again deported. But his rebellious ideas
continued to spread. To ensure against further propagation he was
moved again, this time to a remote settlement only a hundred miles
from the Arctic Circle. Here he wrote his *Life of Archpriest Avvakum*

---

7. Afanasy Nikitkin, *Voyage Across Three Seas,* trans. S. Z. Apresyana (Moscow:
State Publishing House of Geographic Literature, 1960), pp. 107–108, 110, 114.

by Himself, and when it became clear that exile was a poor weapon against this persuasive priest, he and three followers were burned at the stake in 1682.

The *Life* is an extraordinary document—the first Russian manuscript written in colloquial language rather than the more formal Church Slavonic. Ironically, by his use of the vernacular, this powerful advocate of the church's traditions was himself contributing to their decline. Avvakum was the precursor of Alexander Pushkin, the nineteenth-century poet who broke with yet another literary tradition to write in the language of the people and make himself more widely read and understood.

While Avvakum was writing his autobiography in exile, the Russian theater was born in Moscow. Morality plays and puppet shows had been seen in Russia for many years. But the first comedy, complete with stage, sets, props, and curtain was performed before an audience of one, the Czar Alexei, in October 1672, more than fifty years after the death of the English playwright, Shakespeare. The impresario was the German minister of the Lutheran church in Moscow and the story was based on the biblical tale of Esther. A special theater was built in the czar's residence, and the theatrical arts thus gained a special association with the royal court. No public theaters came into private hands until 1882. Foreign companies, mostly Italian and French, were invited to perform in the czar's theater and their styles dominated Russian drama until the end of the nineteenth century.

Avvakum could not comment on the new entertainment from his cold and distant retreat, but before he left Moscow he did remark on the fact that "in many of the churches at Moscow they sing songs instead of sacred chants, . . . wave their hands, shake their heads, and stamp their feet as do the Latin organists."[8]

The new manner of singing, rather than chanting, had come to Russia from Kiev and specifically from the Roman Catholic church whose influence was felt in Kiev while the city belonged to Poland and Lithuania.

Over the centuries, Russian church music had followed the Byzantine monodic, or single voice, pattern, while the Roman church de-

8. Miliukov, *op. cit.*, p. 104.

veloped polyphonic singing: the joining of two musical lines in harmony. The Roman melodies were novel also because they were often derived from folk songs. Ukrainian singers from the region around Kiev thus introduced Western harmonies to Russia and laid the foundations for nineteenth-century Russian orchestral music.

When Peter the Great undertook his campaign of Westernization, he did away with the need for such indirect influences. After his own tour of exploration in Western Europe in 1697–1698, he imported talent directly from the West.

3. St. Petersburg: A Window on the West (1713-1918)

S T. Petersburg, Russia's window on the West, was created by Peter the Great in an effort to liberate landlocked Russia from the vast and frozen stretches of European and Asiatic continents. By establishing the new capital on a northern seaport, Peter not only brought Russia closer to the West, but also brought the West nearer to Russia.

It was through St. Petersburg that hundreds of artisans, dancers, musicians, writers, painters, potters, art dealers, and jewelers were funneled into Russia, bearing the ideas and wares of the West.

The "window" had a screen, however, with which the czars tried to sift out political ideas. The government encouraged cultural imitation to promote learning and technology without allowing in the freer political ideas that might have let the art take root and flourish. The same problem, the desire to limit imitation of Western civilization to certain cultural forms so as not to undermine the Russian political system, still confronts the leaders of Soviet Russia today.

The eighteenth century was one of intense absorption of Western ideas—in modes of dress, language, literature, art, and music. Noble

26

St. Petersburg. *The Bettmann Archive*

families that had at first resisted Peter's Western orientation spoke
only French by the end of the century and were often illiterate in
Russian. Families that began the century afraid that they might, in
dress, be mistaken for foreigners were, by the end of the century,
much more embarrassed about revealing their Russian and peasant
ancestry. And they imported French, English, and German tutors
for their children.

The nineteenth-century poet Pushkin was to mock this contradic-
tion of Russians living in Russia and speaking only Western languages:

> Tatyana read no Russian journal,
> She did not speak the language well
> And found it rather hard to spell;
> And so of course the girl decided
> to write in French. . . . What's to be done?
> For lady never, no, not one,
> Her love in Russian has confided;
> Our native tongue turns up its nose
> At mere epistolary prose.
> They say the ladies should read Russian,
> But though the arguments are keen,
> I cannot suffer the discussion—
> To find a Moscow magazine
> In those white hands would be distressing!

Pushkin further noted that the young ladies were:

> . . . inclined to stammer
> When they employed the mother-tongue;
> We loved them, though, when we were young
> For just those little slips of grammar;
> The foreign tongue is native to
> Those lovely lips; is it not true?[1]

The heavy emphasis on Western manners among the upper classes soon resulted in a cultural schism in the Russian people—a split much greater than the religious schism of the seventeenth century. The mass of the people came to be "old believers" in terms of custom, costume, and manners, far removed from the "new believers" of the aristocracy. Whereas in earlier centuries the country's culture had been a unifying force built around the Greek Orthodox religion in all its architectural, artistic, and literary manifestations, the Russia of the eighteenth century created two cultures. The nobility ate off china plates, watched opera and ballet, sat for portrait paintings and read French novels. The peasantry ate from wooden tableware, danced to traditional folk songs, collected crude woodcuts, and attended traveling circuses.

Yet, despite the outward aping of foreign fashions, Russia's elite lived in a political system that lagged far behind Western Europe's. Murder and coups d'état that had been common in France and England in the sixteenth and seventeenth centuries remained the essential methods of determining the Russian line of succession. The opening to the West was led by the strongest Russian leaders of the eighteenth century, Peter the Great and Catherine the Great. But in spite of their fascination with European ideas, they never allowed the concept of constitutionality to interfere with their own political goals. Peter had his own son killed out of fear that he would lead an insurrection against the throne. Catherine seized the throne from her own husband and then ordered him murdered.

Peter's grandiose plans to build his capital on desolate swampland

---

1. Avrahm Yarmolinsky, ed., *The Poems, Prose, and Plays of Pushkin* (New York: Random House, 1936), pp. 171–172.

Peter the Great founding St. Petersburg. *The Bettmann Archive*

required the skills of European architects and artisans. The construction preoccupied the new capital's sovereigns throughout the century and kept the foreigners coming.

The character of the new city was shaped by Peter's determination to build a fireproof city, by his memories of the cities and palaces he had visited in Europe, as well as by the styles familiar to the architects he imported. He chose a generally low profile, in imitation of Amsterdam. To guard against fire, he copied the stone facades of Western Europe's buildings, and when stone ran out he covered wood and brick with plaster. Because St. Petersburg was located in a swampy region, most of the stone had to be brought over long distances. In addition, all ships coming from Lake Ladoga were required to carry stone as ballast. But still the supply ran out. In

1714 Peter prohibited the use of stone elsewhere in Russia. To fulfill his dream, he also conscripted tens of thousands of serfs to drive piles into the marsh, to haul stones, and build his palaces and canals. Thousands of noblemen and their families were drafted to run the government and populate the new city.

St. Petersburg was further distinguished from wooden Moscow by having an architectural plan in which even the kinds of houses to be built were specified: small ones were to have at least four windows and medium-size ones sixteen windows facing the street; larger ones would be two stories high. The height limitation endowed the city with a low skyline occasionally broken by tall thin church spires which Peter had no doubt admired on his trip to London.

The Russians so identified with the white-trimmed, painted stucco buildings, as in the Italian manner, that they assumed they had originated the style themselves. In 1839 a Frenchman touring Russia met a Russian who insisted he had seen nothing new in Italy. "How could you expect that inhabitants of Petersburg and Moscow would be amazed by Italian architecture like other people?" the Russian

The Hermitage, St. Petersburg. *The Bettmann Archive*

remarked. "Do you not see models of this architecture at every step you take here, even in our smallest villages?"[2]

These simple houses were complemented by grandiose palaces. Peter had been enthralled too by the baroque style of the French kings' residence at Versailles, which he had duplicated in the building, gardens, and fountains of his summer palace, Peterhof. His daughter Elizabeth, though, preferred the French rococo style with its ornamented facades, and one of her successors, Catherine the Great, insisted on the more formal classical Roman architecture.

The magnitude of Peter's will and achievement was recorded by the poet Pushkin in 1833 in a long poem:

> A century—and that city young.
> Gem of the Northern world, amazing,
> From gloomy wood and swamp upsprung,
> Had risen, in pride and splendor blazing.
> Where once, by that low-lying shore,
> In waters never known before
> The Finnish fisherman, sole creature,
> And left forlorn by stepdame Nature,
> Cast ragged nets—today, along
> Those shores, astir with life and motion,
> Vast shapely palaces in throng
> And towers are seen: from every ocean,
> From the world's end, the ships come fast,
> To reach the loaded quays at last.
> The Neva now is clad in granite
> With many a bridge to overspan it;
> The islands lie beneath a screen
> Of gardens deep in dusky green.
> To that young capital is drooping
> The crest of Moscow on the ground,
> A dowager in purple, stooping
> Before an empress newly crowned.
>   I love thee, city of Peter's making.[3]

Peter's grandeur was to be immortalized in bronze as well as words. It is from a statue that Catherine the Great commissioned by the

2. Custine, *Journey for Our Time*, p. 331.
3. Yarmolinsky, *op. cit.*, p. 96.

French architect Etienne-Maurice Falconet that Pushkin took the title of his poem, "The Bronze Horseman." Falconet depicted Peter in flowing cloak astride a rearing horse, placed on a thousand-ton boulder. Peter's expenditure of manpower in the building of St. Petersburg was repeated in this monument to him. It took four hundred men almost two years to move the boulder across the gulf from Finland.

Falconet spent eleven years in Russia and left four years before the statue was completed, embittered by the poor quality of the workmanship and by the squabbles over wages due him. Financial difficulties with the rulers were not unusual for the artisans of the time. Elizabeth I and Catherine II overcommitted even their enormous resources and still overburdened their artisans. The architect Rastrelli refused to ready the Winter Palace bedroom wing for Elizabeth's occupancy until he was paid. The hatmakers and jewelers of Paris shut off her credit and halted deliveries.

Among the famous foreign architects to work in St. Petersburg were Tressini, Schluter, Leblond, Quarenghi, and Rastrelli. Rastrelli was actually a Russianized Italian since his father, a sculptor, had prolonged a three-year commission into a lifelong stay. The work of the foreigners was to some extent affected by their Russian assistants who conveyed to them the Russian passion for columns and windows as decorative elements, rather than just utilitarian structures.

Foreign influences extended to Russian painting as well. The shift from religious paintings to more humanistic subjects had begun in the previous century. Throughout the eighteenth century portraiture was the dominant art form. The czars established a drawing school and eventually an academy of fine arts, mostly staffed by foreign artists, and Russian painters traveled abroad to study. In her desire to establish herself as an enlightened and cultured monarch equal to Western rulers, Catherine purchased huge quantities of Western paintings. Her agents—including the French encyclopedist Diderot —bought entire collections that she never saw until they arrived at the St. Petersburg docks. These wholesale purchases became the sovereign's personal collection and formed the core of the famous Hermitage Museum which was opened to the public in 1852. It was not until 1898 that the czars thought well enough of Russian art to add a section of domestic works to the exhibit.

The bronze statue of Peter the Great by Falconet over-looks St. Petersburg. *Sovfoto*

In music, too, the dominant influences were Italian and French. Italian operas and French comic operas were imported. Playing a classical instrument came to be regarded as a patrician avocation. Examples were set by Empress Elizabeth who secretly married a Ukrainian chorister and bandore player, and the emperors Peter III and Paul I who played the violin.

An imperial ballet school was established in 1738, and its instruction fluctuated between the Italian school which favored acrobatics, and the French school which emphasized more graceful steps. Impetus for the ballet came unexpectedly from the world of fashion. When Peter the Great decreed Western styles for the nobility, he freed them from their floor-length robes and heavy boots and opened the way for frock coats, knickers, and shoes that made dancing much easier. And the ladies who had not previously participated in social events, according to Oriental custom, now became ballroom dancing partners.

From Czar Alexei on, Russian rulers were interested in and promoted the growth of a national theater. In 1750 Elizabeth signed an order permitting dramatic presentations in private homes—that is, in the homes of noblemen. Six years later she established a state-subsidized Russian theater of comedies and tragedies, to be open to the public and to feature plays written, acted, and directed by native artists. The theater's first annual subsidy was only five thousand rubles, although French and Italian companies received four and six times as much. This was the same kind of partiality that czars in previous centuries had shown to foreign painters and architects.

Two men inspired Elizabeth's generosity. One was Alexander Sumarokov (1718–1777), a graduate of the Academy of the Nobility, a playwright and poet whose plays were presented by the military cadets at the academy. The first director of the Russian theaters, Sumarokov was in the forefront of those who broke with the rigid rules of classical poetry and used elements of folk tales and song in his work. The other was Feodor Volkov, son of a merchant from the provincial town of Yaroslavl. In his enthusiasm for the theater, he converted a barn into a theater, trained actors, and achieved such renown with a morality play, *The Repentance of a Sinner,* that Elizabeth requested its performance at court. He remained in the capital, working with Sumarokov in the new theater, and arranged a two-week pageant for Catherine the Great after she ascended the throne.

Support of the theater was maintained by Catherine the Great who built a large theater, established an imperial theatrical school and an administration of theaters, which controlled all dramatic, opera, and ballet companies and orchestras. Catherine herself was not a passive observer of the cultural scene but wrote plays and opera librettos. By the end of the century theatrical enterprises had spread from St. Petersburg and Moscow to the provinces.

In order to staff their private theaters noblemen trained serfs in ballet, opera, and theater arts. Count Peter Sheremetev built on his estates three theaters beautifully designed and decorated by Italian architects. He was an aesthete with a genuine interest in artistic events. With the special approval of Czar Paul, he married one of the serf-actresses.

But not all serf-actors were treated so well. As slaves, they were often whipped for poor performances or sold as pieces of property, which they were held to be by law. Ads in the St. Petersburg *Gazette* read: "Sixteen-year-old peasant girl for sale, well behaved, price 20 rubles," or "Excellent conductor, price 800 rubles."[4]

4. Pierre Descarques, *The Hermitage Museum, Leningrad* (New York: Harry N. Abrams, 1961), p. 21.

As in the other cultural realms, imperial interference in literature spearheaded progress. Peter the Great authorized the first of several reforms of the Russian alphabet, correcting and simplifying it to promote literature and relieve it of church domination. He also edited the first public newspaper and arranged for the translation of many books into Russian.

The century's outstanding intellectual was Mikhail Lomonosov (1711–1765), a writer, educator, and scientist amounting to a Russian version of the Renaissance man. Lomonosov carried forward Peter's linguistic reforms. His *Grammar* laid the basis for a Russian language independent of the religious language known as Church Slavonic. He defined three literary styles: a lofty style for heroic poems, still using Church Slavonic; a middle style for satires and prose writings, using modified Church Slavonic; and a low style for songs, comedies, and epigrams, permitting ordinary or everyday Russian words and syntax.

His achievements led to the formation of the University of Moscow, in 1756, as a successor to the Slavonic Greek-Latin Academy that Lomonosov had attended by hiding his peasant origin. The university, with modern scientific departments, was further proof that the old religious traditions were being supplanted by secular and modern branches of knowledge.

Besides working as a physicist, mathematician, chemist and geographer, Lomonosov wrote poetic odes glorifying the state, its rulers, and its history.

Most fiction produced in the eighteenth century was written in verse. Prose writing, in short stories and novels, did not become popular until the nineteenth century.

But the poetry changed over the years. The odes of Gavriil Derzhavin (1743–1816), a civil servant under Catherine, also glorified her regime, but they were often witty or satiric, and included veiled criticism of imperial power and policies.

Derzhavin's criticisms were even more explicitly rendered by Alexander Radishchev (1749–1802), the first Russian radical writer, whose name today still inspires Soviet authors when they protest censorship and autocratic rule. Radishchev was educated in Europe, where he encountered and adopted the new ideas about personal rights and freedoms. Catherine herself had espoused some of these ideas when she first came to the throne, but she rejected them when they threatened to undermine her authority.

On his return to Russia, Radishchev became a government official and collected experiences about Russian life, published as a *Journey from St. Petersburg to Moscow* in 1790, after the start of the French Revolution. The book condemned many aspects of imperial rule, including literary censorship. It portrayed the corruption of official life—the sale of judicial decisions and the trade in serf-mistresses among nobles. It inveighed against the mindlessness of the bureaucracy. In the tradition of Russian protest writings, Radishchev took the position that Empress Catherine was not informed about these abuses and was kept ignorant of them by her noble entourage. Radishchev used this device to avoid a direct—and impermissible—attack on Catherine. Almost two hundred years later it was used again, often sincerely, by intellectuals who could not believe that Stalin knew of the purges and other outrages committed by his regime.

Radishchev's objective appraisal of his peers extended even to that jack-of-all-intellectual-trades, Lomonosov. Although he acknowledged Lomonosov's contributions to Russian poetry, he criticized the scholar's standardized rules for writing poetry. "Lomonosov," he noted, had recognized "that our verses were ridiculous in Polish dress and stripped them of this unbecoming vestment. He created good exemplars of the new verses and saddled his followers with his great example, and so far no one has dared to depart from it."[5] In this remark Radishchev, who wanted to experiment with new poetic devices, pointed up the difficulty of breaking with tradition in Russian society, perhaps in all society.

Radishchev's book closed with the line, "With the permission of the Department of Public Morals," but actually he had not obtained permission to publish his uncensored manuscript. Disregarding the censor's deletions, he printed the book on his own press and then submitted it to the police, who gave their approval without re-examining it.

Catherine, who had time to act as her own supreme literary censor

5. A. N. Radishchev, *A Journey from St. Petersburg to Moscow,* trans. Leo Weiner. Ed. and with an Introduction and Notes by Roderick Page Thaler (Cambridge, Mass.: Harvard University Press, 1958), p. 191.

in addition to conducting two wars and the affairs of state, discovered this subterfuge. She wrote ten pages denouncing Radishchev as "infected and full of the French madness," and for "trying in every possible way to break down respect for authority and for the authorities, to stir up in the people indignation against their superiors and against the government."[6]

Catherine's fear that revolution would spread from France caused her to have Radishchev arrested, tried, and sentenced to death. She finally banished him to Siberia, but he was freed seven years later by Paul I and recognized as a reformer by Alexander I. Eventually he was named to a commission to revise the civil code. His idealism was shattered when he realized that serfdom would not soon be abolished, and he took his life.

The contest between Catherine and Radishchev, between head of state and an artist, was to be repeated in succeeding centuries when Nicholas I acted as literary advisor and censor to the poet Pushkin, and yet again when Communist party leader Nikita Khrushchev personally screened the writings of Alexander Solzhenitsyn. Westerners can only marvel at the time spent by Russian political leaders in approving and censoring literature. But this is an important clue to the relationship between the Russian artist and the Russian state. Whatever the form of government, czarist or Communist, literary criticism of society was seen as posing a serious political challenge to the ruling elite.

Radishchev's experiences in exile were also echoed in subsequent centuries. Exile, then and now, meant banishment but not always imprisonment in a labor camp. Radishchev was a widower and his wife's sister followed him to Siberia with two of his children. They married and had three more children there. Through the intervention of friends during the next ten years, Radishchev was allowed to take long walks and hunting trips. But he remained isolated from the mainstream of Russian life.

Shevchenko and Chernyshevsky were among the many writers exiled to Siberia in the nineteenth century. Under the Communists, in the twentieth century, the poet Osip Mandelstam was deported to Siberia with his wife. Thirty years later, in the 1960s, Andrei Al-

6. *Ibid.*, p. 239.

marik, writer-historian, was sent to Siberia for two-and-a-half years, where he was joined by his future wife. Later, Almarik worked as a shepherd and cart driver to support himself and his wife.

Thus did Radishchev's career anticipate the trials of many Russian artists. More important, his use of literature as a weapon of protest raised a standard for many writers in the centuries that followed.

The nineteenth century (1800–1917) brought the evolution of a uniquely Russian culture. After borrowing and assimilating Western ideas for centuries, the Russians now produced works of art in all fields that not only augmented their national heritage but also added greatly to the world's cultural reservoir. The poetry of Pushkin and Lermontov, the novels of Gogol, Dostoevsky, Turgenev, Tolstoy, and Chekhov, the music of Moussorgsky, Rimsky-Korsakov and Tchaikovsky, the ballets of Petipa, Fokine, and Diaghilev, the paintings of Repin and Kandinsky, and the theater of Stanislavsky offered instruction and entertainment to a universal audience. By the end of this period, in the early 1900s, the world was beginning to borrow from Russia: Diaghilev toured Western Europe and brought with him Stravinsky's music, Benois' backdrops, and the stars Pavlova and Nijinsky; Tchaikovsky conducted his music in America.

At the start of the nineteenth century most creators of art were nobles, although the performers continued to be serfs. They were amateurs in the sense that they did not depend on art for their income. It would have been difficult to regard art as a profession because society was only beginning to accept the idea that nobles as well as serfs could play musical instruments. Moreover, in previous centuries art had been supported and patronized by the court, so that there existed no independent outlets, such as museums or theaters.

It was not until 1852 that Czar Nicholas I opened the imperial art collection in the Hermitage as a public museum. Privately owned theaters open to the public were not allowed until 1882. Because they lacked the means to reach a large public, and because that public could not in any case grow until serfdom was abolished in 1861, the artists devoted themselves to entertaining their friends at soirées.

Provincial noblemen flocked to the capital city of St. Petersburg where they could find court patronage and aristocratic salons, schools, Western ideas, literary journals and court-supported theaters for plays, operas, and ballet. But proximity to the court also had its drawbacks. Fearing the czar's personal wrath for an unwise decision, the censors in St. Petersburg were more restrictive and the newspapers were more conservative than elsewhere. By the second half of the century, Moscow became an equally popular haunt of the artists and ceased to be snobbishly dismissed as "provincial." Beside the classical stone and stucco architecture of St. Petersburg, Moscow's traditional wooden houses and narrow streets seemed old-fashioned. But it was in Moscow that a class of merchants flourished who eventually became the patrons of Stanislavsky's innovative theater, of a native Russian art, and of French impressionist painters. Here too was born a Russian national music school. The slow shift of cultural activity from the nobility to the middle and lower classes also produced a shift of locale as cultural leadership was divided between the two cities.

By the middle of the century more of the artists came from lower economic and social groups. They were known as *raznochintsi,* "men of different ranks." It was now quite proper for noblemen to be professionally dependent on the arts, but most still came to music or literature after training in some other work. After the abolition of serfdom weakened the nobility's economic base, a job in government or military service was often essential until some generous patron or patroness of art appeared. Not until the end of the century did the working class yield such artists as Gorky and Chagall.

As the social origin of the artists changed, so did the themes of their work: Pushkin's superfluous man, a nobleman useless to the world around him, would appreciate Chernyshevsky's activist revolutionary hero and be repulsed by Gorky's downtrodden outcasts.

The broadening of the social base from which artists evolved, and the subsequent diversification of subject matter, led to a more critical examination of Russian life. Generally speaking, nineteenth-century Russian literature was tragic and pessimistic. It was preoccupied throughout the century with the concept of the superfluous man, the educated but restive and bored aristocrat who is discouraged by custom from taking meaningful action to enrich himself or society. The model for the superfluous man was first drawn by Alexander Griboyedov (1795–1829) in his poetic comedy *Woe from Wit*. His hero, or perhaps anti-hero, is a fellow full of progressive ideas but impotent in politics as in love.

In addition to limning portraits of the unhappy nobleman, writers drew the attributes of the fawning provincial gentry, the domineering patriarchal merchants, and the uneducated, wily peasant.

The literature also reflected the intellectuals' frustration with the country's political system and their conviction that, without revolution, none of the czars would reform or revitalize the country. Serfdom continued to exist until 1861; autocracy until 1917.

Russia's performance in several wars had a major effect, too, on the mood of her artists and the themes they chose. Russia's defeat in the Crimean War in 1856 led to the abolition of serfdom and a brief wave of optimism; her defeat in the Russo-Japanese War in 1904 set off the Revolution of 1905 and produced a period of repression and pessimism; her humiliation in World War I sparked two revolts in 1917, one overthrowing czarist autocracy and the other establishing the Communist regime that was to prescribe a whole new mold for art and artists.

But censorship, the secret police, exile, and forced labor were all features of Russian life and Russian cultural life long before communism. The so-called Section III, or secret police, was an office in Nicholas I's private chancellery. It had charge of the suppression of "un-Russian activities" and "anti-national ideas" and employed spying, secret denunciation, surveillance, investigation, and "administrative measures" such as imprisonment and exile. The officers of Section III, aided by a special body of censors, controlled practically all political life. "In their zeal to justify their existence, the censors committed stupidities," writes one historian. "In a textbook on physics the expression 'forces of nature' was banned as atheistic, while in a cookbook the sentence, 'free air is necessary for cookies,' was suppressed because of its symbolic meaning. A poet who confessed that he cherished his beloved 'above everything in the world' was severely reprimanded by the censor: 'No law-abiding citizen ought to put anything above God and the emperor.' "[7]

To confound the censors, writers often used Aesopian language—

7. Marc Slonim, *The Epic of Russian Literature. From Its Origins Through Tolstoy* (New York: Oxford University Press, 1964), p. 126.

symbolic phrases that only hinted at their real meanings, much as the animals in Aesop's fables were symbolic of real people. Readers became adept at reading between the lines and finding the hidden meanings, but sometimes the language was so burdened by innuendo that it confused not only the censor but also drained the work of literary merit, especially for uncomprehending foreigners.

One custom of Russian writers and musicians was to read or perform their works before other artists at private parties. This was not only entertaining; it served to disseminate literature and music without censorship. Griboyedov's play *Woe from Wit* was read many times at such evenings while he lived, even though it was not approved for public performance until after his death. Throughout the nineteenth century many poets and writers gave private readings. And the tradition has continued into the Soviet era.

Even in its censored form, however, literature assumed an unusual importance in czarist Russia. Lacking free public discussion either in a parliament or in an uncensored press, society relied upon literature for some of its social expression and information. One hundred years later, literature again performed the same function in Soviet Russia, when poets such as Yevtushenko and Voznesensky read their work to huge audiences in public squares and stadiums. Now, as then, the Russians treated poetry as more than poetry. Their literature was their politics.

The political nature of art motivated discussions throughout the century on two sets of questions that still bestir Russian society. The first encompasses the purposes of art: What should be the function of art? Should it be used to educate and indoctrinate people? Or should it be "pure art," without function, striving for new and personal interpretations of reality? And the second set concerned the sources of Russian art: Should Russian art seek its inspiration only in its own history and roots? Or should it be a branch of the world's artistic scene, universal in spirit and appeal?

These questions were and continue to be answered differently by each successive generation of artists.

Literature: From "How It Is" to How to Do It

The Golden Age of Russian literature was inaugurated by Alexander Pushkin (1799–1837), Russia's greatest poet and the author of her first realistic—albeit in rhyme—novel. His greatness lies in the fact that his writings were uniquely Russian in both form and content. Pushkin broke not only with the romantic, Western styles of the English poets, but also with the classical school of Russian literature. His themes were not based on Greek mythology but on contemporary Russian life. His language was the colloquial, everyday language of the Russian people, rather than the stuffy, erudite Church Slavonic that had dominated Russian letters for eight hundred years.

His linguistic achievement was all the more remarkable because most of his tutors and servants spoke only French, German, or English. It was from his nurse that Pushkin learned the Russian language, its folk tales and songs. Though his creative life lasted only about twenty years, he was most prolific. Clear, simple, and original, his short stories and poems remain in the Russian consciousness not only as originally written but also in various reincarnations of opera and ballet.

Alexander Pushkin writing poetry in his room. *The Bettmann Archive*

Pushkin's first long poem, the fairy tale *Ruslan and Lyudmila,* was the inspiration for Glinka's opera of the same name. *Eugene Onegin,* the poetic novel about contemporary aristocratic life, and "The Queen of Spades," a short story about a gambler, were the sources of Tchaikovsky's operas. Other operas inspired by Pushkin poems were Moussorgsky's *Boris Godunov,* Rachmaninov's *Aleko,* and Stravinsky's *Mavra. The Fountains of Bakhchisarai* is the story of a popular Russian ballet by Asafiev, and "Snowstorm" is just one of many stories made into movies a century after Pushkin's death.

Through his mother, Pushkin was descended from the Ethiopian princeling, Hannibal, who was brought to Peter the Great's court as a child. Close ties with the imperial court on both his mother's and father's side helped Pushkin to surmount some of the political difficulties that his work provoked. The young Pushkin's best friends were the future Decembrists, the young officers who tried to seize power from the new czar, Nicholas I, in 1825. Though divided in their political objectives, their agitation anticipated some momentous events of Russian history: the emancipation of the serfs, the murder of the royal family, the abolition of class distinctions, the resort to counterrevolutionary espionage and censorship. Five of the conspirators were hung, in a notable break with the absence of death penalties under Alexander I. The uprising inaugurated a period of oppression that was to dominate the reign of Nicholas I.

Pushkin thus grew up with a keen awareness of political problems, and his early poems dealt critically with serfdom and other policies of the czars. These were seized by the secret police and Pushkin was exiled from the capital to serve with the army in southern Russia. After five years of travel around the south he was eventually ordered to his mother's estate and kept under virtual house arrest for new indiscretions: the police had opened his mail and found assertions of atheistic beliefs.

Through the intercession of older poets, Pushkin met Czar Nicholas I and was again granted permission to live in the cities of Moscow and St. Petersburg with the stipulation that his works would be censored by the czar himself. This proved to be a rather annoying concession since the czar had different aesthetic standards as well as different political views.

After many romances Pushkin finally married. It was not a very happy union and his wife's popularity at court further complicated Pushkin's life; he had to go into debt to maintain her social position.

Trying to ease the financial pressures, Pushkin founded a literary journal in 1836, a year before his death. Though not very successful under his short-lived editorship, the magazine, *The Contemporary,* was to become a prestigious outlet for the century's literature.

Pushkin died of pride and jealousy. Incited by rumors of his wife's friendship with a young Frenchman, he challenged the foreigner to a duel and sustained wounds that killed him within a few days.

Even in death Pushkin's life had creative repercussions. On the day he died, Mikhail Lermontov (1814–1841), a young nobleman, wrote a poem in memoriam to the slain poet. It caused him to be banished, like his idol, from the capital to southern Russia. And, like Pushkin, he died young in a duel fought over a woman.

By the age of fifteen Lermontov was already an accomplished poet, with the main features of his style established. Typical of the young noblemen of the time, he was well educated and knew several languages, including English, and this brought him under the influence of Western literature. Critics have found a resemblance to Byron in his self-characterization as a "persecuted wanderer," his dissatisfaction with life, hypersensitivity, moodiness, and passion.

Careers for young noblemen were limited. Those ranking higher than Lermontov usually were employed at court. For the rest, there was the choice of managing the family estate, government and military service, or indulgence in the trivialities of urban social life. Lermontov went from the University of Moscow to the Imperial Guard Hussars in St. Petersburg, interrupting his writing at first in his desire to be a model officer.

But the muse persisted and the poem in praise of Pushkin led him to be demoted to an infantry division in the Caucasus. In 1839 he was pardoned and again readmitted to the capital where his social successes were matched by his poetic renown. His poems were published in the monthly review, *Notes of the Fatherland,* and he continued to work on his only novel, *The Hero of Our Time.*

The hero, Pechorin, is another figure in the long line of superfluous men that stretches across the Russian literary landscape. They were men, like Griboyedov's Chatsky and Pushkin's Onegin, whose noble birth robbed them of an economic function in society. Born to the highest rung on the social scale, the intellectuals among them were bored and frustrated, denied the need to work and the chance to rule. Pechorin asks: "Why was I born? What was the aim of my life? There must have been an aim, a high destiny, inasmuch as I feel enormous forces in my soul . . . I did not grasp my purpose; I let myself be attracted by the lure of empty and vile passions—and I lost the fire of noble aspirations."[8]

The failure of the Decembrist uprising in 1825 contributed to this atmosphere of frustration, but Lermontov never lost his keen feelings about the inequities and evils of society. Always resentful of his exclusion from the parties of the highest nobility, he was bold in defying their social conventions and their secret police.

In 1840 a duel over a woman resulted in his second expulsion from the capital. As he left for the south, Lermontov remarked: "Farewell, unwashed Russia, land of slaves, of slavemasters, of blue uniforms and of the people whom they rule. I hope that the mountains of the Caucasus will hide me from your pashas with their all-seeing eyes and their all-hearing ears."[9] Shortly after his departure, his novel was published and the censor allowed a collection of poems to be published in book form. A year later, in 1841, he was dead.

Although many contemporaries were quick to recognize the worth of both Pushkin and Lermontov, the typical view of poets at the time was not flattering. When Pushkin died, the acting head of the political police asked: "Why do you make such a fuss about an individual who did not even hold any important post?" And at Lermontov's death another official wondered: "Why do they talk so much about him—after all, he was only a fop, a poor soldier, and a miserable scribbler."[10]

Pushkin inspired others not only with his work, but also his friendship. His friend, Nikolai Gogol (1809–1852), was encouraged and directly motivated by Pushkin in the production of his most famous and remarkable works, *The Inspector General* and *Dead Souls*.

Gogol, the son of a Ukrainian landowner, carried forward Pushkin's literary emphasis on contemporary life. His early stories, drawn

8. *Ibid.,* p. 120.
9. *Ibid.,* p. 116.
10. *Ibid.,* pp. 108, 117.

Nikolai Gogol.
Sovfoto

from Ukrainian folklore, were full of the humor of the rural environment he knew. They also reflected his anxiety about the shallowness of life.

In his story, "The Overcoat," about a poor clerk whose most prized possession is stolen, Gogol depicts one of the now traditional characters of Russian literature: the underprivileged little man who is overwhelmed by the rich aristocrats. Fifty years later, Chekhov was still working the same theme: a clerk accidentally sneezes on the bald pate of a government official and, even though his apologies are accepted, worries himself to death.

This perceptive understanding of personality was exemplified further by Gogol in his other works too. His characters are drawn with so much realistic detail that they almost appear grotesque; it is hard to believe that such insipid, mean, petty, greedy, avaricious people really existed, but yet there they are, vivid and alive.

The significance of Gogol's work, for an influential critic like Vissarion Belinsky (1811–1848), was its purely Russian themes and language. Moreover the author offered not just a documentary account of life, but mixed it with realistic criticism. This style of "critical realism" was a rigorous presentation of the evils and faults of

Russian society; it was to be differentiated a century later from "socialist realism," the Communist doctrine that an author must help his government and society by emphasizing the positive sides of life.

Gogol's inspector-general, Khlestakov, is actually an imposter, who enjoys the tributes of a small town and makes off with its money because it so fears any symbol of authority.

The play was first read at the home of the poet Vasily Zhukovsky (1783–1852). The censors refused to pass it, but Zhukovsky, tutor to the czar's son, arranged for a private reading for the czar, who personally approved a theatrical production in 1836. This was but one of the many times when Zhukovsky interceded for his liberal friends. In 1838, he organized a raffle to buy out of serfdom the Ukrainian artist, Taras Shevchenko (1814–1861), who later became an equally famous poet.

The grotesque humor of Gogol's novel *Dead Souls* is mixed with pathos. The author based his plot on the Russian custom of representing personal wealth not only in amounts of money held but in the number of serfs, or souls, owned. Chichikov is a swindler who wants to make a good marriage by establishing himself as a wealthy man. He travels around the countryside, buying up "dead souls" which he will later mortgage for more tangible wealth. In this portrayal of the Russian gentry, Gogol denounces serfdom and the perversion of morality by a system which condones it.

Gogol's critical realism was representative of much of the literary and philosophical writing in Russia in the middle of the nineteenth century. The desire of the artists of the time to describe the despotic social situation and the arbitrary bureaucracy was summarized by the critic Belinsky like this: "Art for art's sake has never really existed. . . . An art of pure detachment revolving in its own sphere and having no connection with any other manifestations of life is only an abstract dream. . . . He who deprives art of its rights to serve social interests debases the reader instead of elevating him. . . . Today art and literature are more than ever the expression of social problems, and that is the direction in which the Russian natural school is moving."[11]

Some of the new literature appeared in the magazine *The Con-*

11. *Ibid.*, pp. 140–41.

temporary which Gogol had encouraged Pushkin to start. A few years after Pushkin's death, it was purchased by Nikolai Nekrasov (1821–1877), a poet, who disseminated much of the radical thought and great literature of the nineteenth century.

Nekrasov, the son of a nobleman, disinherited for wanting to be a student instead of a soldier, is regarded as a civic poet. His themes dealt with common people, mostly peasants, and their desire for freedom. Influenced by Belinsky, he conceived of the poet as a citizen first, and an artist second, thus exalting the duty of the poet to become involved in the events of his time. This view makes him one of the more popular poets in the Soviet Union today.

As a magazine editor, always in need of good material, Nekrasov became a patron of unknown young writers. When a friend brought him Dostoevsky's *Poor Folk,* his enthusiastic reaction could not be contained until he had awakened the author at four in the morning to make his acquaintance. In 1856 he published Tolstoy's first story, "Childhood," and thus boosted the career of another of Russia's great talents.

Nekrasov yearned for the day when Pushkin's poetry and Gogol's prose could be read by the peasants about whom they wrote. But this was not to happen until the next century when the Soviets made literacy the rule rather than the exception. In the meantime the literature of social criticism was written largely by noblemen and read largely by noblemen.

In 1847 Nekrasov published a short story by Ivan Turgenev (1818–1883), also an aristocrat who wrote objective tales about rural life. Whereas Gogol had concentrated his satire on the gentry who owned peasant-serfs, Turgenev focused on the peasants themselves. His realistic portrayal of the harsh life of the peasant did not fail to show some of the harsh qualities of the peasant himself.

Turgenev was educated in European universities and spent much of his adult life in France. Returning to Russia in 1852, when his *Sportsman's Sketches* was published in book form, Turgenev was placed under house arrest because he was thought to have slandered the landed aristocracy.

The theme of the superfluous man persists in Turgenev; only now the young nobleman is confronted not just by boredom and impotence but also by a general social stagnation.

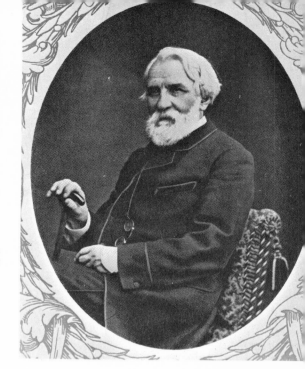

Ivan Turgenev.
The Bettmann Archive

In *A Nest of Gentlefolk*, Turgenev's hero is again a passive type who wishes to help his peasants but in the end lacks the where-withal. *A Nest of Gentlefolk*, like other novels that appeared in the 1850s, was nostalgic about the landed aristocracy, soon to be threat-ened by the freeing of the serfs in 1861. Tolstoy's *War and Peace*, which appeared in 1869, was a more epic depiction of the idyllic life of this class.

The abortive revolutions of 1848 in Western Europe produced a period of special repression in Russia. Czar Nicholas I regarded him-self as the champion of autocracy and the old values. But while de-fending them and seeking for Russia an outlet to the Mediterranean through Turkey's Dardanelles, a crucial forty-mile strait, Nicholas stumbled in 1856 into the Crimean War. The Russians were badly defeated by the French and British at Sevastopol, a Russian naval base on the Black Sea. Nicholas died before the peace treaty was signed, but his son, Alexander II, responded to the cries for reform —stimulated in part by Turgenev's *Sportsman's Sketches*—and abol-ished serfdom in 1861. Legally, the measure freed serfs from bond-age, but it did not directly give them the land they wanted.

The 1860s thus became a decade of great intellectual and social turmoil. Artists scented change and pursued it in their own lives, often demonstrating the qualities they attributed to their new heroes.

The superfluous man, at least for a while, was displaced in literature by the man of action and the emancipated woman. Both shunned their moneyed backgrounds to work for revolutionary change. Turgenev described these types in his novel *On the Eve.* The characters were similar to those in Chernyshevsky's *What Is to Be Done?,* which glorified the purposeful citizen.

In *Fathers and Sons,* Turgenev depicted with great psychological insights the clash between two generations—the fathers of the landed aristocracy and their sons, revolutionary nihilists. Nihilism, a word popularized by Turgenev, was a denial of conventional values (etiquette, dress, language) and traditional institutions (family, church, state) and a substitution of reason or thought as the basis of all action. In their adherence to what they called rationalism, the nihilists were so fanatic and dogmatic that they were almost "irrational." They believed art should propel social change and, in practical terms, they tried to awaken the Russian masses by going directly out into villages to teach and train them.

Most of the Russian populace was illiterate and it was ironic, though also true of other social revolutions, that the fomenters were not the needy but those with enough education to know how to organize and arouse the underprivileged.

The Russian populists—socialists who believed in the inherent goodness of the Russian peasant—imitated some of the techniques of the nihilists. But eventually both groups were disheartened by the ineffectiveness of their programs and the lack of peasant response. To promote social change they now resorted to terrorism, tight revolutionary organization, and plans to assassinate the czar. Many attempts were made on the life of Alexander II and one finally succeeded in 1881. In 1887 an attempt was to be made on his son Alexander III, but it was uncovered by the police. Among those hung for the crime was Alexander Ulyanov, the brother of Lenin who, in 1918, when head of Communist Russia, avenged his brother's death by countenancing the execution of Czar Nicholas II and his family.

Turgenev had always been noted for his gentle, refined language. But the hero of *Fathers and Sons,* Bazarov, eschews niceties of language and manner as conventions of the past. He is thus typical of the nihilists as well as the *raznochintsi*—the new group of writers and intellectuals from nonaristocratic backgrounds. Sons of priests, like Chernyshevsky, or of poor government clerks, like Ostrovsky, their language was coarser and more direct.

The tradition of critical realism was perpetuated by Alexander Ostrovsky (1823–1886), Russia's most prolific playwright. His forty-seven plays constitute a national repertoire, adhering to contemporary Russian language in contemporary Russian settings. His plots and characters are drawn from Moscow's middle-class merchant circle, with which he was familiar.

Though even now not well known in the West, Ostrovsky remains the most frequently performed playwright in the Soviet Union. Typical of many nineteenth-century artists, Ostrovsky did not educate himself for a literary career. He attended law school at the University of Moscow and then became a clerk in the local courts. When his plays were read at Moscow's literary salons, he was forced to resign his job and to write to support himself. Typically, too, Ostrovsky had trouble both with the police and the censors. His plays, by their powerful representations of merchant mores, so offended Moscow merchants that at one point the censor refused to approve the production of one of his plays for twelve years.

Ostrovsky's plays dealt with loveless middle-class marriages arranged for money and with domineering patriarchs and matriarchs, whose greed condemned young brides to aged bridegrooms.

Ostrovsky became emotionally involved with theatrical folk as well as with his scripts. His concern for the miserable way in which both actors and playwrights were regarded led him to found organizations to provide for the welfare of the former and to protect the literary rights of the latter.

Despite his social awareness, Ostrovsky was not committed ideologically to either the Slavophiles or the Westernizers.

The Slavophiles, who believed that everything Slavic, and therefore Russian, was superior to anything Western, and the Russian Westernizers, who wished to incorporate other European values and techniques, were both strong nationalists. Both aspired to the goal of Russian supremacy in the world, but their proposed methods for reaching that goal differed. The Slavophiles—"lovers of Slavs"— believed that the radical reforms of Peter the Great, the persecution of those who preferred the old religious orthodoxy, the adoption of

Western clothing and Western hair styles had all been a mistake. Resenting such borrowing and proud of their own past, they felt Russian greatness depended on the preservation of its patriarchal, autocratic traditions.

The Slavophiles were naturally approved of by the czars, but the Westernizers such as Peter Chadayev (1794–1856), Alexander Herzen (1812–1870), and Nikolai Chernyshevsky (1828–1889) were penalized for their views. Chadayev was declared insane and restricted to his house by Nicholas I after a magazine article critical of the autocratic regime was published; Herzen voluntarily exiled himself in England after the European revolutions of 1848 had failed and an atmosphere of repression had set in again in Russia; Chernyshevsky was sentenced to hard labor in Siberia.

The Westernizers' most brilliant spokesman was Herzen—a critic, writer, publisher, and socialist. Like other Europeans of his time, Herzen saw in socialism the political democracy and economic equality that were not available to man when he was ruled by kings and capitalists. He lived the second half of his life in Western Europe, an expatriate, yet still deeply involved in Russian cultural and political life through his magazines, *The Bell* and *The Polar Star,* the first uncensored publications distributed in Russia, although they were published in England. The magazines and other works printed by Herzen's Russian Free Press were smuggled back into Russia and widely read, even at the czar's court. (Today Soviet writers have recourse to similar publications, printed in Western European cities, as outlets for their underground literature. When it re-enters the Soviet Union, the literature is known as *tamizdat*—published over there.)

Herzen used them to condemn all that was backward in Russia and campaigned for free speech, a free press, and the end of serfdom. While the government in power always regarded such criticism as subversive, it was written with a great love for Russia and a desire to improve her life. Many Russian writers were afflicted with this love-hate attitude toward their homeland.

Herzen's vision of a socialist future was a mixture of his Western socialist ideas and his own personal belief that Russian experience with agricultural communes, called mirs, would make her socialism better than the Western kind.

Nikolai Chernyshevsky, an editor of Nekrasov's journal, *The Contemporary*, was an equally brilliant author, critic, and socialist. Arrested for his political views in 1862, he was sent to prison where he wrote *What Is to Be Done?*, a novel urging the emancipation of women, with a rational, deeply committed revolutionary as its hero. In 1863, for no specific offense, he was exiled to prison in Siberia for twenty-one years. Chernyshevsky believed that economics was the basic cause of all oppression, inequality and war, and that public ownership of the means of production under socialism would eradicate these evils. His views were similar to those of Karl Marx and Friedrich Engels, the Western theoreticians of Marxist communism; and Lenin, the leading Russian revolutionary, re-used his title, *What Is to Be Done?* in a famous revolutionary pamphlet in 1905.

Chernyshevsky had belonged to a socialist discussion group known as the Petrashevsky Circle after the name of the man in whose home it met. Among the other members was Feodor Dostoevsky (1821–1881), a struggling young author, educated as a military engineer and the son of an army surgeon of landed gentry. Having abandoned his profession, Dostoevsky supported himself by translating from the French and writing original stories.

Feodor Dostoevsky.
The Bettmann Archive

All the members of the circle were arrested in 1849, although Chernyshevsky managed to escape. While they were awaiting execution of the death sentence, in fact while the first group of prisoners stood blindfolded, expecting a firing squad to take aim, the czar's messenger arrived to announce that they were spared and sentenced instead to four years of penal servitude and four years of military service in Siberia.

The only book Dostoevsky could read in exile was the New Testament, a fact which probably contributed to the religiosity of his future writings. On release from prison in 1854, Dostoevsky wrote to his brother: "My stomach was ruined. I was repeatedly ill. As a result of my bad nerves I became epileptic. And I have rheumatism in my legs. I shall not tell you—it would take too long—what happened to my soul, my beliefs, my mind and heart, during these years. But the constant concentration on my inner self, to which I escaped from bitter reality, bore its fruit."[12]

Eventually Dostoevsky did tell the whole world in a succession of novels that made him one of Russia's most acclaimed writers. The "twisted personality, morbid individualism, and embittered philosophy" of some of his characters were no doubt a reflection of the agonies that Dostoevsky had personally endured. He identified with the downtrodden, poverty-striken hero of his story, *Poor Folk,* who could not escape from a morass of degradation, unhappiness, evil, and corruption. In his *Notes from the House of the Dead,* about the Siberian years, he further describes suppressed people who are deformed by society into inhuman shape. The types of whom he wrote were to arouse the imagination of another Russian, Maxim Gorky, whose own victim-heroes were unable to escape from the economic bondage imposed by society. A hundred years later *The House of the Dead* was to have yet another echo in Alexander Solzhenitsyn's *One Day in the Life of Ivan Denisovich,* a novel about Siberian penal servitude in Soviet Russia.

Like Ostrovsky, Dostoevsky became a professional writer and relied upon his literary production for his earnings. His financial condition was often bleak. This, coupled with ill-fated romances and bouts of epilepsy, caused him to leave Russia twice in the 1860s

12. *Ibid.,* p. 275.

—to escape his creditors, to find time to write, and simply to rest. Abroad, he often gambled and lost heavily, but he turned experience into profit by writing *The Gambler,* a novel.

Dostoevsky dismayed the socialist radicals of the 1860s by his Slavophile sympathies and his religiosity. In *Crime and Punishment,* his central character, Raskolnikov, a nihilist, rationally decides to do good by killing a pawnbroker, an act that dominates the whole novel and eventually destroys its hero. Losing his self-confidence, Raskolnikov succumbs to the love of a religious woman who believes that Christ dominates her desperate, unhappy life. Faith conquers reason. That becomes Dostoevsky's message also in his masterpiece, *The Brothers Karamazov.* It suggests Dostoevsky's belief that personal and national salvation for Russians is to be found in the Orthodox church and in the autocratic state that controls the people's anarchic tendencies. By thus supporting the institutions that radicals were sworn to overturn, Dostoevsky came to be regarded as a conservative and is still honored only reluctantly in Soviet Russia today. But his literary power has been universally admired.

The first Russian author to acquire an international reputation, however, was Leo Tolstoy (1828–1910). His life of eighty-two years extended from a time when the landed aristocracy still stood at the

Leo Tolstoy.
The Metropolitan Museum of Art, Gift of the Sculptor,
1911

zenith of its power to a time when the whole czarist system was breaking down. In those eight decades, Tolstoy searched constantly for the meaning of life and pursued a wide variety of careers—soldier, estate-manager, writer, farmer, educator, philosopher and polemicist. His fame and his accessibility drew to him a large circle of acquaintances, including Ivan Kramskoy and Ilya Repin, the painters; Peter Tchaikovsky, the composer; Anton Chekhov and Maxim Gorky, the writers; Konstantin Stanislavsky and Vladimir Nemirovich-Danchenko, the theatrical directors.

Tolstoy's creative life is easily divided into two periods: the first found him abandoning university study for service as a soldier, traveling abroad, managing his estate and writing the historical epic *War and Peace,* the novel *Anna Karenina,* and other stories based on his own life. The second period encompasses his conversion from organized religion to private religiosity, a kind of primitive Christianity.

The fictional works of this latter period are almost as didactic as the nonfiction. In an essay "What Is Art?" Tolstoy expressed the view that art must serve the people and therefore must be comprehensible and simple, taking the form of folk art, folk tales, or folk music. Though he did not align himself with any political or literary movement, Tolstoy eventually became a movement unto himself, largely as a result of the new way of life he established after his conversion.

Tolstoy was born into a rich, aristocratic family and received the typical training befitting such birth. He learned English, French, and German, which he used on travels abroad in 1857 and 1860. In his late teens and early twenties, still typically, he struggled to avoid becoming a superfluous man. But his initial attempts to elevate the life of the 350 "souls" on his family estate were rebuffed by the suspicious serfs. During his army service he participated in the Crimean War and his sketches about Sevastapol, which developed into a panegyric against war, were severely censored.

Land and the peasantry attracted Tolstoy's energies. Returning from war or European trips, his first thoughts went to the improvement of his estate with orchards and reforestation and the peasants' need for schools or a chance to buy their freedom. He organized a school on the most progressive principles of education and even wrote down simple nursery tales, such as "The Three Bears," for his pupils.

Tolstoy's marriage at thirty-four to the eighteen-year-old daughter of one of the czar's physicians commenced one of the happiest periods in his life. Both husband and wife kept diaries, and each was allowed to inspect the other's. Tolstoy's constant soul-searching and self-analysis, and his extraordinary perceptions as revealed in this diary, enabled him to endow his characters with a unique depth and solidity. Besides bearing him eleven children and helping to manage the estate, Tolstoy's wife assisted in his work by copying all his manuscripts for the printer.

The theme for *War and Peace* was an autobiographical rendering of his family's life during the Napoleonic invasion in 1812. Tolstoy researched family records and government documents and interviewed many eyewitnesses to gain the proper background for the novel. The plots of his other novels and plays were similarly based on real events: *Anna Karenina* was inspired by the suicide of a neighboring landowner's mistress, who had been supplanted by a younger woman; the plots of *Resurrection* and *The Living Corpse* were court cases that had been retold to Tolstoy by friends in the legal profession.

Tolstoy's marriage, a seemingly perfect union of interests, was gradually eroded by disputes that grew out of his spiritual crisis in the late 1870s. The great gulf that eventually separated husband and wife can only be measured by Tolstoy's desperate flight from home one night, which led to his death a few days later.

In his consuming search for the meaning of life and the means to live it well, Tolstoy rejected science and philosophy as unsatisfactory ideals. He chose instead the path of religion and love of God as a way of removing himself from the materialism of life. Kinship with rural surroundings had caused him to seek answers among the peasants, whose calm approach to death was the result of total faith in God.

In time he came to identify almost completely with the peasants' way of life, assuming their faith, their occupation, their dress, but not their organized church. He preached equality, love of man, simplicity in life and material acquisitions, passive resistance to the state's authority. In short, he preached a Christian communism. He saw the outline of a better society not in political movements like socialism, but in individual, ethical renewals of faith. Like the populists, Tolstoy believed that ordinary people were a source of great spiritual strength and that agriculture was the most desirable occupation.

In practical terms, Tolstoy's new ideas led him to renounce the profits from his literary endeavors and to place in the public domain all his work published after 1881. He was one of the few artists who did not just portray life but actually lived the life he advocated. According to a recent biographer, "He humbled himself by hard physical labor, and he practiced what he preached about productive work. He learned from a craftsman how to make boots; he did all the menial work of caring for himself—he swept the floor, emptied the chamber pot, and mended his clothes—he pumped the water for the household and transported it in huge tubs; he worked in the fields, plowing, mowing, lugging manure, felling trees, carting timber, and carpentering."[13]

And yet there was always a central paradox: this life of simplicity was possible for Tolstoy only because of the great wealth he had earlier inherited and accumulated.

While many of Tolstoy's literary productions between 1881 and 1910 are philosophic tracts and political diatribes, he reverted from time to time to writing fiction, almost always in a didactic vein. His play, the *Power of Darkness,* and his novel, *Resurrection,* are social sermons without the romance of the earlier novels.

Tolstoy is still venerated in Russia, not only by the people and for the magnitude of his literary contributions, but also because the Soviet authorities value his credo that art must serve society. His books, sold in millions of copies, have been glorified in plays and movies.

Even on his deathbed Tolstoy continued to inspire artistic creation. Leonid Pasternak, the artist, drew a portrait of Tolstoy at death; Merkurov, the sculptor, made a cast of his head, and photographers memorialized the moment on film.

---

13. Morris Philipson, *The Count Who Wished He Were a Peasant,* a Life of Leo Tolstoy (New York: Pantheon Books, 1967), p. 105.

Music: Songs from the Steppes

The literary development of Russia, which began with the lone, innovative figure of Pushkin and culminated in a surge of work by Dostoevsky, Tolstoy, and Turgenev, was paralleled by a similar development in music. Russian music in the nineteenth century became nationalist in content and form and spawned two warring camps, the Slavophiles—the advocates of realism—and the Westernizers—the advocates of pure or abstract music. The nationalism of the music expressed itself in symphonies, songs, operas, and ballets based on Russian folk music, folk tales, contemporary poetry, or historical events. Its Oriental melodies, reflecting the Russian empire's growth to the Asian west and south, became an obvious trademark by which audiences around the world identified Russian music. Most importantly, the new music broke with the classical Italian forms and ignored the work of most contemporary European composers, such as Wagner.

Its realism was expressed in program music. Program music usually has a specific title and follows an identifiable story line, such as Tchaikovsky's *1812 Overture* or Moussorgsky's *Pictures at an Exhibition*. The concert audience was given a printed program explaining the development of the music, to make it more understandable. In this way, program music resembled civic literature or the realist movement in art; its purpose was to create real musical images, rather than abstract sounds.

The herald of the new musical nationalism was Mikhail Glinka (1804–1857), son of a wealthy landowner. Like many of his musical heirs, he was an amateur composer who came to music accidentally, and had very little formal instruction. Prevented by his father from going directly into a musical career, Glinka first joined the Ministry of Communications in St. Petersburg. But his heart was not in that work and at the first opportunity he resigned to return to his musical dabbling. His interest in music had been inspired by the private orchestra of an uncle, and he studied with its musicians and took piano and singing lessons from the European teachers in the capital.

Glinka's poor health was the excuse for a trip to Western Europe, where he spent several seasons absorbing Italian opera and studying composition in Berlin from a German master. The immersion in Italian music was enough to convince him, however, that he wanted to compose something particularly Russian. He wrote to a friend, "The most important point is a well-chosen subject. In every way it will be absolutely national. And not only the subject, but the music."

Glinka succeeded in this aim in his first opera, *Ivan Susanin*. The story dealt with a peasant who saves the life of the first Romanov czar by deceiving the Polish soldiers who pursue him. The plot was suggested by the composer's friend, the poet Zhukovsky. Predictably, this patriotic theme pleased the czar, who attended one of the opera's rehearsals. Its title was changed to *A Life for the Czar*, so as to glorify the czar instead of the peasant hero, and it became a frequent candidate for performance on imperial feast days. Eventually it came to be used to inaugurate each season at the Bolshoi Theater in Moscow, a custom still observed today in the Soviet Union. The Soviets, in their turn, have reverted to the opera's original name so as not to be reminded of their political predecessors.

Typical of the theatrical conditions that prevailed until the 1880s, Glinka's opera first went into rehearsal not in a state theater, but in the private home of a prince. The head of the imperial theaters was invited to listen to a performance of the first act and agreed, after much persuasion, to accept the opera for public performance on the condition that Glinka take no fee.

The opera, performed in 1836, was enthusiastically received. Glinka's goal of a purely national music was only partially achieved—the opera was a blend of Italian form and German harmony, mixed with Russian folk songs. But the czar liked it so much he gave Glinka an expensive ring and later appointed him master of the imperial choir.

Glinka wrote one other opera, based on Pushkin's *Ruslan and Lyudmila,* but it brought him only grief. He had trouble finding a librettist. Although the quality of the music surpassed that of *A Life for the Czar*, it was expressed in a new Russian idiom and left audiences pining for the more familiar Italian characteristics to which they had become accustomed. One grand duke admitted that when he sent his soldiers to hear it, it was punishment, not reward. After that first season it was not performed again for twenty-one years.

Discouraged, Glinka went abroad and spent the rest of his career traveling, disengaging from an unhappy marriage, looking after his poor health, and composing some symphonic pieces based on folk songs and a few smaller works.

Of one of these symphonic folk songs, the "Kamarinskaya," Tchaikovsky later wrote that "the present Russian symphonic school is all in 'Kamarinskaya' just as the whole oak is in the acorn . . . from 'Kamarinskaya' all later Russian composers (including myself) draw contrapuntal and harmonic combinations whenever they have to deal with a Russian dance tune."[14]

Alexander Dargomyzhsky (1813–1869) was Glinka's successor in bearing the new national musical tradition. He copied the notes Glinka had made from German theory lessons and wrote two operas emphasizing the dramatic quality of the story, which he felt Glinka had ignored.

Dargomyzhsky thus embraced the general interest in realism that dominated Russian art between 1850 and 1870. But his art was not immediately accepted. As Dargomyzhsky wrote, "My position in St. Petersburg as an artist is not an enviable one. The majority of our amateurs and newspaper scribblers do not think I am inspired. Their unimaginative ear demands melody, and that is not my object. I have no intention of lowering the level of music to entertainment in order to suit them. I want sounds to express words directly. But this is beyond their comprehension."[15]

Dargomyzhsky was saying that the words of an opera were as important as the music. He was carrying forward the program music that dominated composition throughout Europe, some of which fitted into the tradition of "critical realism"—program music with not only a story but a message, as in Moussorgsky's *Songs and Dances of Death.*

Modest Moussorgsky was one of the five members of a loose association of young musicians known as the Mighty Five, who often met at Dargomyzhsky's home. Their leader was Mily Balakirev (1837–1910), about whom Glinka wrote to his niece: "No one else

14. M. D. Calvocaressi and Gerald Abraham, *Masters of Russian Music* (New York: Alfred A. Knopf, 1936), p. 62.
15. Miliukov, *Russian Culture*, vol. III, p. 110.

Modest Moussorgsky.
Sovfoto

has ideas so like my own. One of these days he will be a second Glinka."[16]

Mily Balakirev wrote only one symphony in addition to some smaller works, but he contributed enormously to Russian music as teacher and critic to his friends and pupils, Cesar Cui, Nicholas Rimsky-Korsakov, Alexander Borodin, and Moussorgsky.

Except for Balakirev, who briefly studied mathematics at Kazan University but then devoted himself fulltime to music, these men had looked upon music as an avocation originally. Cui was trained as a military engineer, Rimsky-Korsakov as a naval officer, Borodin as a doctor and chemist, and Moussorgsky as an army officer. None had any formal academic instruction in music. They learned from private piano lessons, associations with private orchestras, and from Balakirev. Balakirev was a generous but tyrannical teacher. Rimsky-Korsakov recalls that "he held us absolutely spellbound by his talents, his authority, his magnetism. He appreciated even the faintest signs of talent but anything he disapproved of he would tear to pieces and hold up to derision so remorselessly that often his vic-

16. Calvocaressi and Abraham, *op cit.*, p. 60.

tims, humiliated and angry, were led to renounce him for a time, if not for ever."

But he also was a molder of musical taste. According to Rimsky-Korsakov, "The group favoured Glinka, Schumann, and Beethoven's last quartets. Beethoven's symphonies, except the ninth, were considered relatively insignificant; Mozart and Haydn, antiquated and naive; Bach frigid and mechanical. Balakirev used to compare Chopin to a 'nervous society lady.' Liszt's music was unknown, and dismissed as jerky and perverse."[17]

Balakirev had played in and conducted a private orchestra in his native town of Nizhni Novgorod and learned at first hand the classical scores of Mozart and Beethoven. The private orchestra was one of the few ways for an aspiring musician to explore live music since there were few public concerts of serious music. Although schools for painting and architecture had existed in the capital since the middle of the eighteenth century, there was no institution for formal music instruction until 1862. With Balakirev as teacher and Victor Stassov, the famous music critic, as mentor, the Mighty Five dedicated themselves to the creation of a national school of Russian music, independent of Western influences. They carried into music a general reaction to the West, a kind of feeling that "we are old enough to do it ourselves."

Of the five, Moussorgsky, Borodin, and Rimsky-Korsakov were the most gifted musicians. They could write all kinds of music, but they are renowned for their program music—operas, songs, and ballets.

Moussorgsky (1839–1881) is best known for his two operas, *Boris Godunov* and *Khovanschina,* and for his songs. *Boris Godunov,* based on the Pushkin poem and the writings of Karamzin, a Russian historian, recounts the events of the so-called "time of troubles" at the beginning of the seventeenth century when false pretenders were claiming the Russian throne. *Khovanshchina* describes the seventeeth-century conflict between the government and the people over religious reforms.

Though he had carefully researched his historical material, Moussorgsky had great difficulty getting the operas produced. Depressed,

17. *Ibid.,* p. 114.

often drunk, poor and ill, he died at age forty-two, before he had a chance to orchestrate the piano score for *Boris Godunov.* Even after Rimsky-Korsakov wrote the orchestral parts, the imperial theaters refused to produce it for more than a quarter of a century.

Moussorgsky's interest in painting led to friendships with various artists. The world's impression of Moussorgsky will always be colored by Ilya Repin's portrait of him in his hospital room a few days before he died, sitting in his robe, looking agitated. Painting inspired the piano score *Pictures at an Exhibition,* which Moussorgsky wrote after touring a memorial exhibition of the artist Victor Hartmann in 1873. This too was later orchestrated by Rimsky-Korsakov. Each of its ten episodes recreates the mood of a different painting, as Moussorgsky tried to paint with notes instead of shapes.

Moussorgsky first met Alexander Borodin (1833–1887) when they served in a military hospital, Moussorgsky as an officer, Borodin as a doctor. Borodin was an impressive figure, pursuing the twin careers of research chemist and amateur composer with equal international success. In his memoirs Rimsky-Korsakov describes Borodin's skill in juggling his two interests: "He knew almost as little as I did about orchestration generally, but a little more of its practical side, since he could play the flute, the oboe, and the 'cello. I often found him at work in his laboratory, whence he would lead me to his rooms. But even in the midst of playing or talking, he would jump up all of a sudden and fly to his retorts and burners to make sure that all was well—filling the air, as he went about, with incredible sequences of ninths and sevenths, bellowed at the top of his voice."[18]

Borodin, troubled by the demands on his talents, wrote to a friend, "So far I have felt shy of letting it be known that I am engaged on an opera. My real business, after all, is scientific work; and I feared lest by concentrating too much on music I discredit that work. . . ."[19]

Borodin had been introduced to music at military band concerts and his first lessons were from the band's flutist. From this modest beginning came three symphonies, an opera, and other orchestral pieces. His music is perhaps the closest in spirit to Glinka's, and Russian audiences found it just as new and dissonant and hard to listen to.

18. *Ibid.,* p. 162.
19. *Ibid.,* p. 169.

Borodin's opera, *Prince Igor*, like Moussorgsky's, was built on a historical theme—a twelfth-century prince's unsuccessful campaign against a Turkic tribe (see pp. 10–11). Borodin died before he finished the opera or his Third Symphony. Rimsky-Korsakov (1844–1908) completed the unfinished scores, as he had for Moussorgsky, this time with the aid of Alexander Glazunov (1865–1936).

Rimsky-Korsakov wrote the first Russian symphony, but he is far better known for his operas, most of them on Russian themes, and for his symphonic suites, such as *Scheherezade*. Stumbling on a musical career through a chance acquaintance with Balakirev, he nonetheless stayed in the navy for many years.

By chance, too, while still in his twenties, Rimsky-Korsakov was offered the post of professor of practical composition and instrumentation at the St. Petersburg Conservatory. He was urged to take it by Balakirev, despite his ignorance of the subject, so as to gain a foothold in that prestigious institution. Rimsky-Korsakov admitted that "It was not merely that I couldn't at that time have harmonized a choral properly, had never written a single contrapuntal exercise in my life, and had only the haziest understanding of strict fugue; but I didn't even know the names of the augmented and diminished intervals or of the chords. . . . And so undeservedly given a professorship in the Conservatory, I soon became one of its best pupils—perhaps the best of all—as regards the quantity and quality of the knowledge that I acquired there."[20]

Though still an "amateur," Rimsky-Korsakov at one point was simultaneously teaching at the Conservatory, serving as inspector of naval bands, and directing the Free Music School. In addition, he conducted concerts and kept on composing.

But his fame in Russian music rests also on his service as executor of the musical estates of his friends. After Dargomyzhsky's death, he orchestrated his opera, *The Stone Guest,* and oversaw its production. His friendship with Moussorgsky, with whom he had roomed for a year, and Borodin, whom he visited frequently and constantly goaded to work, inspired him to complete their major unfinished works. He knew their music intimately because the composers had played their works to each other and performed the piano versions of symphonic

20. *Ibid.,* pp. 356–57.

pieces at private parties. When operas were "tried out" in this informal way, each guest sang a role.

Rimsky-Korsakov's music was not rated as profound as the operas of Borodin and Moussorgsky, but the nationalistic qualities of his works endear him to Russian audiences. His operas based on the tales of Pushkin, Gogol and Ostrovsky were embroidered with folk songs which he had learned from his mother and uncle. Borodin's peasant maid also helped him with the collection of *One Hundred Russian Folk Songs,* which he completed in 1877.

The death of Borodin in that year, following several years after Moussorgsky's death and the nervous breakdown of Balakirev, continued the dissolution of the Mighty Five. Rimsky-Korsakov found a new circle of musical friends in the home of M. P. Belaiev, a rich man greatly interested in chamber music. Out of Belaiev's musical suppers grew a music publishing house, a fund for destitute musicians, a series of symphonic concerts, prizes for orchestral works, and chamber music competitions—in all of which endeavors Rimsky-Korsakov was an active adviser. Among the members of this new circle were some of Rimsky-Korsakov's former students, Alexander Glazunov and Anatoly Lyadov.

The government also helped to subsidize well-known musicians by offering them the post of director of the imperial chapel. Glinka had once served as music director of its choir and the managership and musical directorship passed in the 1880s to Balakirev and Rimsky-Korsakov.

But such official recognition of their musical standing did not automatically extend to all their work. The opera librettos of Rimsky-Korsakov had to be approved by a dramatic censor, who often raised difficulties because the stories were political or pictured royalty in a bad light. The fate of Rimsky-Korsakov's *Maid of Pskov* illustrates the problem. In the opera, the Pskovians, who had a republican constitution, had to be represented not as a free people defending their rights but as rebels. In addition, there was the delicate question of the characterization of Ivan the Terrible, since Nicholas I had decreed in 1837 that while it was permissible for members of the house of Romanov to be represented in plays, they could not be portrayed in operas. Singing was too undignified for a czar, it seemed. This same sensitivity about royal ancestors was shown by the reaction of the grand dukes Vladimir and Michael to *Christmas Eve,* an opera based on a Gogol story. They complained that a backdrop painting of the Petropavlovsk Fortress, in which their ancestors were buried, had desecrated their royal memories, and that Catherine the Great was being "impersonated" by a singer.

Throughout the last quarter of the century Russian composers traveled back and forth to Western Europe, performing and advertising their new music, often to a warmer reception than at home. The Mighty Five had thus become acquainted with the music of Berlioz, Liszt, and Wagner but, for the most part, their music remained immune to these influences. They insisted on being Russian and on making Russian music different from all others.

Rimsky-Korsakov, the youngest of the five, was destined to become a link between the Russian school of music and the Western, cosmopolitan group that was headed by the brothers Anton and Nikolai Rubinstein (1835–1881).

Anton Rubinstein (1829–1894) had also studied musical theory with Glinka's German mentor. But Rubinstein wished to perpetuate in Russia the broad stream of Western music—its harmonies, symphonic forms, and chamber music as then understood through the works of Mozart, Beethoven, and Brahms. In 1859 Rubinstein organized the Russian Musical Society and conducted its concerts. In 1862 he founded in St. Petersburg the first Russian music conservatory. In 1866 his brother organized a similar institution in Moscow.

To compete with these pro-Western institutions, Balakirev set up the Free Music School in 1862. It offered performances of the "modern" composers of the Russian school.

The Mighty Five usually stood apart from Peter Tchaikovsky (1840–1893), one of the first graduates of the St. Petersburg Conservatory who was thus regarded as a member of the cosmopolitan camp. Yet, like the Mighty Five, Tchaikovsky had been destined for a career in government service and, along with them, he felt the attraction of Russian folk melodies.

After graduating from the School of Jurisprudence, Tchaikovsky worked in the Ministry of Justice as a clerk. But the piano lessons that he received as a child had sparked an early interest in music. Now, through an aunt, he was introduced to the world of opera. Stimulated by these experiences, he enrolled in the newly-opened conservatory,

Peter Tchaikovsky.
Sovfoto

devoting himself more and more to music and finally resigning from his clerkship. To support himself, he joined Nicholas Rubinstein at the new Moscow Conservatory as a professor of harmony, and he gave private lessons.

Tchaikovsky did not firmly side with either camp in the great musical controversy. The Mighty Five recognized much of his work as genuinely Russian and performed it at their concerts, while his supposed allies, the brothers Rubinstein, often denounced it.

Of the major Russian composers, Tchaikovsky wrote the largest number of pieces in the greatest variety of styles. He wrote symphonies, operas, ballets, orchestral suites, concerti, overtures, cantatas, and string quartets. Schooled, as the Mighty Five were not, in the theory and orchestration of music, he was not limited as some of them had been by lack of technique.

But he was emotionally unstable, subject to depressions whenever he felt unappreciated. He was given to trickery to win contests and secrecy to obtain new instruments sooner than his rivals. He traveled abroad to escape a Russia that he felt did not love him enough, then returned, sick with longing for home. He made surreptitious plans to attend the premieres of his symphonies in St. Petersburg, then stayed away because he feared the public reaction. He spoke of loneliness and his need for marriage, then fled from his wife after only a few months. Some of these problems were alleviated, others exacerbated by the events of 1877.

Early in that year, a wealthy woman, Nadejda von Meck, volunteered to become Tchaikovsky's patroness, first offering disproportionately large sums for commissioned works, later settling on him an annual stipend. It was to be one-third of Tchaikovsky's income. That spring Tchaikovsky seemed to fall in love with Tatyana, the fictional heroine of Pushkin's poem *Eugene Onegin,* about which he was writing an opera.

Disclosing her love for Onegin, Tatyana wrote him a letter in which she declared:

> I write you, and my act is serving
> As my confession. Why say more?
> I know of what I am deserving—
> That you should scorn me, or ignore.
> But for my wretched fate preserving
> A drop of pity, you'll forebear
> To give me over to despair . . .
> Another! . . . No, I could have given
> My heart to one, and one alone!
> It was decreed . . . the will of Heaven
> Ordains it so: I am your own . . .
> So be it! Now my destiny
> Lies in your hands, for you to fashion;
> Forgive the tears you wring from me,
> I throw myself on your compassion . . .
> Imagine: here I am alone,
> With none to understand or cherish
> My restless thoughts, and I must perish,
> Stifled, in solitude, unknown.
> I wait: when once your look has spoken,
> The heart once more with hope will glow,
> Or a deserved reproach will show
> The painful dream forever broken![21]

21. Yarmolinsky, *Pushkin,* pp. 174–76.

With such lyrics on his mind, Tchaikovsky received a love letter and invitation from a former student which, contrary to his custom, he decided to answer in person. The outcome of the meeting was a decision to marry her, probably brought about by his feelings toward the fictional Tatyana and his desire not to be like the cold, heartless Eugene. He became afraid of scorning the young girl, explaining in a letter to Mrs. von Meck that "I saw that I had gone too far and that if I now suddenly turned from her, I should make her really unhappy and drive her to a tragic end. I was faced with an unpleasant alternative: either I must keep my freedom at the cost of a human life, or I must marry. There was nothing for it but to choose the latter course."[22] Tchaikovsky married the girl to keep her from suicide, then toyed with suicide for himself and fled. With the help of his brother and Nikolai Rubinstein, he was formally separated from his wife, who later died in an insane asylum.

Tchaikovsky's music passionately reproduced all this tension and gradually changed from objective and abstract styles to deeply emotional moods. People came to identify the melancholy of his music with the "Russian soul," but it was much more nearly Tchaikovsky's soul that they heard crying out. Of his last symphony, Tchaikovsky wrote: "The symphony will be called simply 'Programme Symphony' (No. 6). This programme is subjective through and through, and during my journey while composing it in my mind, I often wept bitterly."[23] On his brother's suggestion, however, Tchaikovsky did title the symphony *Pathétique*.

In his later years, Tchaikovsky lived in the country near Moscow, but he came out of isolation periodically for triumphal tours of Europe and even the United States.

Tchaikovsky ended up blending together the two dominant currents of his musical age. The Slavophile current is present most noticeably in his Second Symphony, which begins and ends with folk-song themes, and in those operas which are based on Russian stories, such as *Eugene Onegin* and *The Queen of Spades*. At the same time, Tchaikovsky's work embodied many of the modes of

---

22. Calvocaressi and Abraham, *op. cit.*, p. 292.
23. *Ibid.*, p. 330.

Western music which he had absorbed in his years at the conservatory.

By thus bridging two worlds, Tchaikovsky cleared the way for a new group of composers, the most famous of whom produced work unmistakably Russian and yet simultaneously in the forefront of Western musicology: Igor Stravinsky, Sergei Rachmaninov, and Sergei Prokofiev.

Another span in the bridge linking the Russian and Western traditions was the personal one forged by Rimsky-Korsakov. By outliving the rest of the Mighty Five, and by remaining an active music teacher, he exercised great influence on the next generation of composers. One of his most famous students was Igor Stravinsky (1882–1971).

Stravinsky's childhood resembled that of most upper-class Russians—winter in the city, summer at the country estate, nurses who acted as parents, and parents who were like visitors to the nursery. The first opera he attended—Glinka's *A Life for the Czar,* in which his father sang a leading role—made a vivid impression. He later wrote: "His orchestration . . . remains a perfect monument to musi-

Igor Stravinsky at the piano, with German composer Wilhelm Furtwangler at right.
The Bettmann Archive

cal art—so intelligent is his balance of tone, so distinguished and delicate his instrumentations; and by the latter I mean his choice of instruments and his way of combining them. I was indeed fortunate in happening upon a *chef d'oeuvre* for my first contact with great music. That is why my attitude toward Glinka has always been one of unbounded gratitude."[24] Despite his father's career in music, Igor's parents decided that he should attend law school. But this did not deter him from seeking a musical career and taking lessons from Rimsky-Korsakov.

Stravinsky left Russia in the early 1900s to work with Serge Diaghilev in his Russian ballet company. Stravinsky then wrote three ballets—*Firebird, Petrouchka,* and *The Rites of Spring*—that reflected the newest polytonal and polyrhythmic ideas, and yet retained Russian themes.

After the Revolution of 1917, Stravinsky was joined abroad by other emigrés, among them Rachmaninov and Prokofiev. Rachmaninov was a brilliant pianist as well as composer and had gained fame as the conductor of the Imperial Grand Theater and Philharmonic Orchestra in Moscow. He is best known for his piano concertos. Prokofiev's music was broader in scope than Stravinsky's and more original than Rachmaninov's—full of melody and buoyant and spontaneous rhythms which were often humorous as well. Though he rarely departed from the traditional tonal system, his music was forward-looking and moved all music into another era.

Art: Painting It Like It Is

Russian painting was also caught up in the search for a new spirit of nationalism, and for new forms of social criticism. Though it did not achieve the originality of literature and music which attracted worldwide recognition, it did steer Russian painting onto a more modern course. But first, it had to break loose from the classical, romantic, and noncontroversial traditions of the old-fashioned academy, which dominated the field through most of the nineteenth century.

24. Arnold Dobrin, *Igor Stravinsky, His Life and Times* (New York: Thomas Y. Crowell, 1970), p. 10.

The Major's Wooing, a painting (1848) by Paul Fedotov. *Sovfoto*

The academicians had stressed themes from the Bible, from mythology and from the baroque Italian art that they saw at the Hermitage Museum in St. Petersburg. Students who pursued the prescribed program were rewarded with gold medals and trips to Western Europe.

The first Russian painter to diverge from the rules of style and theme was Alexei Venetsianov (1780–1847). Studying the Dutch and French genre painters[25] of the eighteenth century, he longed to work outdoors, in natural light and with real live subjects. Though he portrayed people in a stylized, idealized manner, he did turn Russian art toward recognizable Russian scenes.

A geodesist by profession, Venetsianov resigned from his job to paint in the open air in the country. His paintings were purely pictorial, that is, they did not attempt to tell a story or convey a point of view. Essentially, they offered a glorified view of peasants walking horses in a field, nursing their babies, or sitting on a threshing floor.

25. Genre painting is the realistic portrayal of everyday life.

But it was to be just another short step to the work of Paul Fedotov (1815–1853), who tried to portray real life, through a more critical eye. Never trained by the academy, Feodotov showed that it was possible to paint without certified credentials.

His most famous work, poking fun at the military, and entitled *A Newly Decorated Knight,* showed a disheveled officer the morning after he received his first medal. The omnipresent censor, afraid of offending the upper classes, refused to allow the picture to be lithographed until the medal had been removed and the title had been changed to *The Morning after a Party.* In other pictures, Fedotov satirized an elderly officer courting the daughter of a rich merchant, and a fallen aristocrat, living in poverty, while an advertisement for oysters lies near him on a chair. Fedotov did not bother to go outdoors for inspiration. His Gogolesque satire lampooned the domestic life of the bourgeoisie. But there was no doubt that he had contemporary Russian reality in his view.

Two events radically changed the art world in the 1840s: the St. Petersburg Academy of Arts closed down its boarding section, its well-disciplined young students metamorphosing into arty bohemians, and a school of painting, sculpture and architecture was established in Moscow. The Moscow art tended to be more free and experimental.

The era of social criticism or ideological realism was inaugurated by Vasily Perov (1833–1882), who, though he did the usual stint abroad for a few years, returned to Russia and devoted his artistic life to studies of the lower class. While Fedotov had satirized the bourgeoisie, Perov criticized the rural clergy and depicted the poor in general.

The biggest break with tradition occurred in 1863, when thirteen students of the St. Petersburg Academy refused to accept the mythological subject of *Odin at Valhalla* as the theme for the Gold Medal Contest. Influenced by the revolutionaries of the day, especially by Chernyshevsky who advocated the use of art as a social weapon, the students quit the academy, organized their own cooperative to sell their work and then, in 1871, established themselves as the Society for Traveling Art Exhibitions. Colloquially, they came to be known as the Wanderers. With the help of P. M. Tretyakov,[26] a

26. In 1892 Tretyakov donated his collection of Russian art to the city of Moscow. It is still housed in a gallery bearing his name.

wealthy Moscow merchant and art patron, the Wanderers organized exhibitions of their works in many parts of Russia.

The leader of the rebels and founder of their society was Ivan Kramskoy (1837–1887). Having worked as a retoucher of photographs before attending the academy, he brought a strong yearning for realism to his four hundred portraits.

Ilya Repin (1844–1930), perhaps the most famous of the Wanderers, painted portraits and scenes from history. But he is best known for scenes from Russian life: men pulling heavy barges along the Volga River, political prisoners awaiting death, a family's reunion with a father returning from exile in Siberia. His historical works, like the one showing Ivan the Terrible grieving over the son he had killed, also imply criticism of tyranny.

Repin was a neighbor of Tolstoy and often sketched the writer in his home, in the forests, and in the fields. One of his famous oils is of Tolstoy, dressed in peasant hat and boots, plowing his field.

Tolstoy's opposition to war, aroused by the Crimean War in which he participated, was shared by one of his disciples, the artist Vasily Vereshchagin (1842–1904). Traveling with the Russian army during the campaign to conquer Turkestan and during the Russo-Turkish war, Vereshchagin depicted not the glory of war, but its horror. His pictures inspired several of the songs in Moussorgsky's *Songs and Dances of Death*. Criticism of his war paintings by generals and by the czar was so intense that Vereshchagin burned some of his work, including the one that had most inspired the composer. Vereshchagin remains best known for his illustrations of Tolstoy's *War and Peace*.

While some artists used realism to look anew at the life around

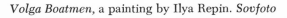

Volga Boatmen, a painting by Ilya Repin. *Sovfoto*

them, others adapted the new style to a more nationalistic portrayal of Russia's past. One of these, Vasily Surikov (1848–1916), was a descendant of Cossacks who conquered Siberia. He attended the St. Petersburg academy but exhibited his large historical canvases with the Wanderers. Repin and Kramskoy were among his friends.

Surikov's interest in the past was aroused in his Siberian home town, filled with old relics, architecture, and costumes. On his way west to the academy he stopped and explored in some of Russia's oldest cities, Yaroslavl and Vladimir. His scenes from history were huge; *Yermak Conquers Siberia*, for instance, measured almost nineteen feet by nine feet—and took years to paint. Like Repin, Surikov studied historical sources, such as costumes in museum collections and Siberian chronicles, to find material for his paintings.

The outstanding feature of Surikov's paintings was the mass of people that he moved around his canvases. Yet each figure among hundreds was unique, drawn by the artist from live models. In describing the characters in *The Execution of the Streltsi*—the czar's palace guard—Surikov wrote, "Remember the *strelets* with the black beard? That's Stepan Fyodorovich Torgoshin, my mother's brother. As for the women—we had grannies like them in our family. The old man in the *streltsi* is an exiled convict of seventy. I met him once staggering under the weight of a heavy sack, and bowing to the people in greeting. The redheaded strelets is a gravedigger I saw at a cemetery. . . ."[27] Even in recalling the past, Surikov relied on the present. One of the most dramatic of Surikov's paintings was the *Boyarinya Morozova,* a depiction of the arrest of one of the most ardent supporters of the Old Believer religious sect. In another, he painted Stenka Razin who led a peasant uprising in the seventeenth century. Probably Surikov was choosing historical events that glorified not only the Russian past but also those figures in that past who stood for freedom and personal rights against the state.

The more formal paintings of Surikov and Repin had depicted the outstanding events and personages of Russian history. But it was Victor Vasnetsov (1848–1927), son of a country priest, who chose to dedicate his painting to its earliest period—that of the medieval knights. Besides glorifying Russia's early military history in a de-

27. N. Mashkovtsev, *Vasily Surikov*, trans. Lucia Flaxman (Moscow: Foreign Language Publishing House), p. 22.

tailed, realistic style, Vasnetsov painted church interiors and theatrical scenery.

One of Surikov's contemporaries, who was influenced not so much by his historical themes as by his landscape backgrounds, was Isaak Levitan (1861–1900). Today his realistic canvases are among the most popular with Soviet citizens, as are the plays of his close friend, the author Anton Chekhov. Partners in pranks at masked balls, and companions in walks through the woods, they both portrayed the elusive beauty of Russian nature, the one in pictures, the other in words. Chekhov regarded Levitan as Russia's best landscape painter and Levitan once wrote to Chekhov: "I do not speak about the mass of very interesting thoughts, but the landscapes in these tales are the height of perfection . . ."[28]

At one point their relationship was ruptured by Levitan's mistaken belief that Chekhov had caricatured him as the lecherous artist in his story, "The Grasshopper," but they were reconciled. It is probable, however, that an event in Levitan's life—his killing of a sea gull —did inspire Chekhov's play, *The Sea Gull.*

The interest in historical paintings signaled a Slavic revival that also affected the purely decorative and functional arts. Inspired by Chernyshevsky's thesis that "reality is superior to its imitation in art," many artists abandoned their easel painting for a time to turn to applied arts and crafts, even stage design and production. Art henceforth was to be "useful" not only in carrying a social message but also in practical ways.

The revival of old crafts was stimulated also by the new industrialism of Russia and the desire to protect and perpetuate the old hand crafts against the challenge of the machine. Workshops and craft centers were formed by aristocrats and merchants in an effort to revitalize these skills. Pottery, embroidery, and textile printing were encouraged at the estate of the Princess Tenisheva and with even greater success at Abramtsevo, a country house near Moscow, where Gogol had once worked.

In the 1870s Savva Mamontov, a railway tycoon, purchased Abramtsevo and, with his wife, then indulging an interest in reli-

28. Ernest J. Simmons, *Chekhov: A Biography* (Boston: Little, Brown, 1962), p. 87.

gious revival, decided to build a church for the village peasants. Among the artists who were lured to work at Abramtsevo were Victor Vasnetsov, Maria Yakunchikova, and Mikhail Nesterov. The reconstruction of the wooden church inspired them to do research and to hunt for carved wooden objects in nearby cities. It led to the design of a mosaic floor, the embroidery of the altar cloths, and the painting of the walls. After the church was completed in 1882, Mamontov's workshops at Abramtsevo continued to produce pottery, with designs supplied by contemporary artists such as Vrubel.

Intense interest in Russia's past also led to the establishment of an archaeological society and to scholarly studies of icon painting and of the popular wood blocks known as *lubok*. And there was a revival, among city people, of folk instruments such as the balalaika, gusli, and dombra.

Lubok were inexpensive, crudely drawn woodcuts and lithographs that had become popular with the masses in the seventeenth century. They portrayed fables or current events—such as the czar's officer cutting off a reluctant nobleman's beard—and mocked upperclass society. In response to Western cultural influences, secularization, and the decline of the icon, some icon painters switched to this new mode of expression. By the end of the nineteenth century surviving icon painters were reduced to bartering their work for butter and eggs. (Ironically, their skills were saved from extinction by the anti-religious Soviet government which diverted them to the production of lacquer ware—black papier-mâché boxes decorated with delicate scenes from Russian fairy tales. Other iconographers were used to restore icons in the Kremlin churches, now treated as museums.)

Concurrently there developed an industry devoted to new and contemporary decorative art. Jeweled easter eggs fashioned by Karl Fabergé, a St. Petersburg goldsmith, came to be regarded as the highest expression of artistic interest in the eighteenth-century art of France. Fabergé, of French Huguenot and Estonian descent, was asked by the Emperor Alexander III to design a gift for his wife. The first egg was presented in 1884, and like the more than fifty that were produced in subsequent years, it contained a surprise: either pictures of the imperial family or a small object, such as a detailed, jeweled model of a Trans-Siberian express train. Fabergé jewelry was presented annually by the czar to actors and ballet dancers in

An eighteenth-century Russian snuffbox of gold and enamel. *The Metropolitan Museum of Art, Gift of J. Pierpont Morgan, 1917*

Inside this Fabergé Easter egg is a folded model of the first Trans-Siberian Railway train. *Novosti from Sovfoto*

the imperial theaters. To qualify for the crown and double-headed eagle pins, the actor had to appear in at least three summer productions in the czar's private theater.

Styles in painting, prose, and poetry tend to move in cycles, reacting to contemporary politics as well as to the styles of the recent past.

Mikhail Vrubel (1856–1911) personified this trend by trying consciously to break away from the realist tradition and establish a more personal art. He is the forerunner of the "art-for-art's-sake" movement that began to develop at the end of the nineteenth century as a response to the socially useful spirit in art in the 1860s and 1870s. Vrubel's art was decorative, often employing color and form for their own value. He thus stood among the antecedents of the abstract and wholly unrealistic painters who would soon emerge in Russia and throughout Europe.

Also formed at this time was the World of Art group, St. Petersburg's "cosmopolitan" answer to Moscow's Slavophilism. The older, interior capital tended to concentrate on the traditional arts whereas the newer, more western capital longed to import the contemporary trends of the West.

Like the Wanderers and the musical Mighty Five, the World of Art group was a distinctive association of artists. It was begun in the 1890s in St. Petersburg by a group of students, several of whom were of Western European descent. The group wanted not so much to invent new artistic techniques as to serve as a funnel through which Western work and styles could pass into Russia. Organized by Alexander Benois (1870–1960), who became a painter, theatrical designer, producer, scholar, art critic, and historian, the group included a former music student of Rimsky-Korsakov, Serge Diaghilev.

The society argued that art existed for art's sake, not for religious, political, or social propaganda. Among all Western styles, it had a special nostalgia for eighteenth-century French art—which had been so influential in St. Petersburg during the reign of Catherine the Great—and an enthusiasm for French late nineteenth-century art—Impressionism.

The society organized annual exhibitions of Russian and Western art, beginning in 1899, and lasting until 1922. It also published for six years a magazine, *World of Art,* which covered events in all fields of art.

The most dynamic—though as a practitioner of the arts, the least talented—member was Serge Diaghilev (1872–1929). He began by organizing exhibitions of British water colors and Scandinavian art in St. Petersburg, then created the society's magazine and went on to become one of the world's most enterprising impresarios in all the arts.

For several years he worked for the Imperial Theater Administration, editing their theater annual and producing, in 1901, the ballet *Sylvia,* in which he utilized atmospheric decor in place of the more realistic, traditional settings. A dispute with the theater administration led to his resignation and his attention turned toward other Russian arts, although he subsequently made ballet production his life work.

Diaghilev's antiquarian interests were realized in an extraordinary exhibit of Russian eighteenth-century portraits, in 1905, which he arranged in St. Petersburg's Tauride Palace, the first exhibit ever held there.

A year later, now in Paris, Diaghilev scored another first, by staging a complete exhibition of Russian art, from the earliest icons to the latest nineteenth-century works. Parisians were introduced to Russian music through concerts Diaghilev organized in 1907. He produced Moussorgsky's opera, *Boris Godunov,* at the Paris Opera in 1908. A year later he brought a whole season's worth of Russian ballet productions to Paris, thus inaugurating his Ballet Russe.

Diaghilev's enterprise and energy united Russia's greatest artistic efforts. For his ballets, he used not only existing music, such as the Polovtsian Dances from Borodin's opera *Prince Igor,* but he also commissioned music by new, young composers, notably Stravinsky.

On leaving Russia Diaghilev took with him the artists Bakst, Golovin, and Roerich to design his sets, and the star dancers Anna Pavlova and Vaslav Nijinsky. The troupe was reinforced each year by other leading performers in the St. Petersburg ballet world, such as Tamara Karsavina.

Russian ballet began as an imitation of dancing in Italy, where ballet originated, and France. The dominant choreographer at the

A costume study by Léon Bakst for Nijinsky in his role in a ballet. *The Metropolitan Museum of Art, gift of Sir Joseph Duveen, 1922*

imperial ballet school in St. Petersburg in the nineteenth century was Marius Petipa (1822–1910), a Frenchman who spoke no Russian. He created seventy-four main ballets in the conventional European tradition.

His successor, Mikhail Fokine (1880–1942), aspired to a more

Anna Pavlova.
Sovfoto

Mikhail Fokine.
Novosti from Sovfoto

natural style, mixing free movements with the traditional toe dancing, and substituting short dramatic routines for the classical three-
and-four-act stories in dance. Most of all, Fokine strove for consistent
presentations. He found it odd that artists playing Egyptians wore
curled mustaches, according to the contemporary hair styles, or
that the traditional short ballet dress, rather than long loose tunics,
should be worn by dancers impersonating ancient Greeks. He objected to full-length ballets, which had begun with Tchaikovsky's
The Sleeping Beauty, because they were padded with extraneous
numbers, such as Slavic dances, which were irrelevant to the plot. To
integrate the performances, Fokine had to overcome the resistance of
the bureaucracy of the imperial theaters and also of the dancers
themselves.

Although the dancers in government-sponsored theaters enjoyed
a guaranteed income, their salaries were not very high. The men
especially augmented their incomes by giving private dancing lessons. Since it was the fashion for teachers to appear at their students'
homes in evening dress, they insisted on wearing that dress to rehearsals, thus upsetting Fokine's costuming plans. What is more,
whenever rehearsals ran long, they criticized Fokine for impinging
on their incomes.

Fokine, therefore, was frequently tempted to join Diaghilev's Paris
ballet company where he found the same emphasis on integrated
productions, combining the best of music, art, and dance.

Under the czars petitioners for admission to the ballet school were
judged on physique, beauty, and singing ability. From the second
year students lived at the school. Performances were given on
Wednesdays and Sundays with the younger students appearing in
groups in the last act and the older students dancing small individual
parts. The curriculum, to Fokine's dismay, lacked any courses in the
history of ballet, painting, or drama. At his suggestion a course in
aesthetics was introduced.

Upon acceptance in the ballet company each dancer was guaranteed an income for twenty years after graduation and a life pension.
The ballet world thus offered security and fame, and dancing became one of the earliest artistic professions in Russia. Under Petipa
and Fokine ballet became a popular spectator sport. Claques formed

in support of certain dancers and devoted fans refused to give up their theater subscriptions from one generation to another.

These traditions of partisanship and sportslike enthusiasm persist among ballet lovers in the Soviet Union today. Those who love Maksimova, loathe Plisetskaya; others feel just the reverse. Both dancers prosper. Although ballet was not native to Russia, it has been developed there to a perfection that evokes universal admiration.

1900–1917: Up and Out

The impulse to unite different art forms for a more complex and exciting theatrical experience gripped another impresario of the time, Savva Mamontov, the owner of a Moscow opera house and the sponsor of the Russian craft revival at Abramtsevo.

Mamontov's opera was one of the first privately-owned commercial theaters in Russia and set a standard for artistic originality. It led the way in coordinating high quality music, costumes and scenery with the main business of singing and dancing, thus helping to break down some of the oldest conventions of the imperial theaters. And it had an enormous influence on nonmusical drama by firing the imaginations of the founders of the Moscow Art Theater, Konstantin Stanislavsky and Vladimir Nemirovich-Danchenko.

Konstantin Stanislavsky in a scene from Gorky's *The Lower Depths. Tass from Sovfoto*

Russian stagecraft was primitive at the end of the nineteenth century. As in the opera and ballet, much attention was paid to the main performers, but little thought was devoted to the sets and properties. Furniture was placed in rigid patterns, without regard to the action on stage. No real stage props were used, since trees and other objects were usually painted on the standard backdrops. Costumes existed in only three categories: Italian, Spanish, and French.

Although more attention was paid to acting, it, too, was confined by conventional, classical rules. There were prescribed gestures for every emotion—for instance, a hand over the heart meant great pain —which evoked standardized responses from the audience.

A new direction for the Russian theater, which was to have repercussions throughout the Western theater world, was charted by Konstantin Alexeyev-Stanislavsky (1863–1938).

He took the name Stanislavsky from an old Polish actor so as to achieve a separate identity from his famous industrialist family, the Alexeyevs. Like Mamontov, whose entrepreneurial interests developed from training as a singer, Stanislavsky's zest for the theater was nurtured in family theatricals and amateur groups. He organized an acting society in 1888 in which he directed and acted, and ten years later, with Vladimir Nemirovich-Danchenko (1858–1943), founded the Moscow Art Theater. Responsibilities in this joint venture were shared: Nemirovich-Danchenko, a playwright and drama teacher, scouted for new plays and supervised production; Stanislavsky directed and acted. Both men, especially after they had been exposed to a German touring troupe, the Meiningen players, were imbued with a desire to reform the Russian theater and to make the drama more realistic. They also aspired to integrated productions, in which realistic settings, costumes, music, and props would all enhance the moods created by the actors.

The problem that most absorbed Stanislavsky was the theatrical definition of reality. At first he emphasized natural settings and acting styles. He banished the programmed gestures of the Italian theater and insisted on comfortable, everyday movements. To promote an easy naturalness, he made actors preparing to play in *Julius Caesar* walk around Moscow for days in Roman togas so that they would effortlessly handle the draping of the garment. For its props for

Russian historical plays, such as Alexei Tolstoy's[29] *Czar Feodor*, the theater's first play, the company scoured the countryside for real wooden cups, spoons, and cloths, and what it couldn't find it copied from exhibits and records in museums. For contemporary plays, such as Ibsen's *Hedda Gabler*, furniture was brought from Ibsen's Norway.

The changes made a powerful impression on the opening night audience. Stanislavsky's stress on the natural was so great that critics often quipped that his stage nights were so dark nobody could see a thing. It was certainly true that Stanislavsky did not hesitate at anything to promote "reality"; his actors even turned their backs to the audience!

His methods soon posed the philosophic question of whether drama should appear to be merely a slice of life, accidentally observed by the audience, or whether it should be deliberate "show," exaggerating real life, and departing from it, for the instruction and entertainment of the people out front. Stanislavsky came to wonder even whether his audiences should merely sit passively in front of his stage or whether they should be made to feel part of the action.

In due course, however, Stanislavsky came to believe that naturalness should be only a tool of drama, and not an end in itself. To promote the search for a more satisfying dramatic experience, he started a branch theater, which was to be the first of several experimental studios. He was inspired by and worked with one of the former actors of the Moscow Art Theater, Vsevolod Meyerhold, who had also been a pupil of Nemirovich-Danchenko. As Stanislavsky records in his memoirs, "It was time for the unreal on the stage. It was necessary to depict not life itself as it takes place in reality, but as we vaguely feel it in our dreams and visions, in moments of spiritual uplift. It was this spiritual state that it was necessary to portray, just as it was shown by modernistic painters on their canvases, by the musicians of the new school in their compositions, and by new poets in their poetry. The works of these painters, musicians, and poets have no clear outlines, no definite and finished melodies, no clear thoughts. The strength of these works lies in the combination

29. Count A. K. Tolstoy (1817–1875) was a distant cousin of Leo Tolstoy, the famous novelist.

of blending of colors, lines, musical notes, and the euphony of words. They create a mood that subconsciously infects the audience. They give hints which compel the spectator to create a picture in his own imagination."[30]

While this studio failed to realize Stanislavsky's hopes, it did help him resolve his inner doubts and allowed him to proclaim what came to be known as his acting "method." It was to have a profound effect on the dramatic art of many Western countries.

In his quest for emotional as well as physical "reality," Stanislavsky wanted to help the actor to "evoke creative inspiration on the stage whenever he wanted to."[31] He felt it was not enough for the actor to create only the external signs of emotion. He had to evoke them internally, too, by concentrated study of the character he was portraying and by liberating himself from his own physical tensions. The spiritual and physical sense of the actor had to be wholly involved in the recreation of another person. By identifying with his character in this way, the actor would force his audience to become emotionally involved with the action.

Through his "method," Stanislavsky added a brand new psychological dimension to acting. In combination with the new "reality" of settings and props, it greatly enriched theatrical experience.

When Stanislavsky took the Moscow Art Theater on tour to Germany for the first time, he joined Diaghilev and others in reversing a trend of centuries and bringing a uniquely Russian art to the West.

A sense of trepidation about its reception gripped the company. It wanted to show the Germans that Russians were talented and not just uncouth Slavs, and that after so many years of borrowing from the West, they now had something to give. Stanislavsky recalls the trip in his autobiography: "The stage hands in the theatre had a rather primitive idea of Russian art. They apparently took us for circus acrobats and wondered why we had not brought along any trapezes. . . . After the Russo-Japanese War and the revolution the treatment of Russians abroad was almost disdainful and it was our mission to try to uphold Russian reputation as much as we could. . . .

30. Konstantin Stanislavsky, *My Life in Art*, trans. G. Ivanov-Mumjiev (Moscow: Foreign Language Publishing House), pp. 334–35.
31. Nikolai Gorchakov, *The Theater in Soviet Russia*, trans. by Edgar Lehrman (New York: Columbia University Press, 1957), p. 33.

We were risking our reputation not only in Europe, but in Russia also, for if we had failed, the Russians would never have forgiven us."[32]

The tour was a great success, as had been an earlier trip to St. Petersburg, which the Moscow troupe approached with almost as much anxiety. "Our fear," Stanislavsky writes, "was due to the fact that there had always been a great deal of animosity between the two capitals. All that came from Moscow was a failure in Petersburg and vice versa. Our fears, however, were in vain; we were received very well. We became good friends with Petersburg and visited it annually after the Moscow season."[33]

Throughout his theatrical career Stanislavsky was plagued by the censors. This was especially true when plays had socio-political significance such as Ibsen's *The Enemy of the People.* Censors attended all the performances and raised a fuss over every extra—or even missing—word.

Despite these handicaps, however, Stanislavsky molded many famous artists, among them the actors and actresses Ivan Moskvin, Vera Komissarzhevskaya, and Olga Knipper, and the directors Vsevolod Meyerhold and Eugene Vakhtangov. He also gave new opportunities to musical talents, such as Alexander Gretchaninov. But, aside from the "method" itself, the Moscow Art Theater's greatest contribution was its production of the work of two contemporary writers, Anton Chekhov and Maxim Gorky.

When Nemirovich-Danchenko won the Griboyedov prize for his play, *The Worth of Life,* in 1896, he remarked that the award should have gone instead to *The Sea Gull* by Anton Chekhov, which had premiered—and flopped—in St. Petersburg.

Within two years, the infant Moscow Art Theater staged the same *Sea Gull* with its new methods and produced a resounding success. Thus encouraged, it produced other Chekhov plays, endowing them with that special psychological quality and dramatic tension that is difficult to find in a mere reading of them. The company's great admiration for Chekhov, cemented most tellingly by the marriage of one of its leading actresses, Olga Knipper, to Chekhov in 1901, was made permanent by its adoption of a sea gull as its symbol.

32. Stanislavsky, *op. cit.,* pp. 338–39.
33. *Ibid.,* p. 283.

This 1958 staging of Chekhov's *The Three Sisters* probably is not much different from the original production by Stanislavsky in 1903. *Sovfoto*

Anton Chekhov (1860–1904) was typical of the new generation of writers who, like Maxim Gorky, rose from humble, lower-class origins. The son of a grocer and grandson of a serf, Chekhov was educated as a doctor. He took his medical degree in Moscow, paying for his education by writing humorous stories. Although he dabbled in medicine all his life, writing soon became his real profession.

Once encouraged to write in a more serious vein, Chekhov produced the short stories and novelettes that brought him the Pushkin Prize of the literature section of the Academy of Sciences, with Tolstoy, in 1900. His once comic stories became increasingly more melancholy. They were almost plotless glimpses of life, as caught by a camera, revealing the sadness and sordidness of Russian life, peasant or gentry. Their inconclusive endings evoke a poignant sense of futility. They are about adultery ("The Lady with the Dog"); about educated young people who must return to the boring life of a country estate ("At Home"); about a young girl who marries a much older man ("Anna on the Neck"); about a prosperous shopkeeper who is turned out of his house and left destitute by his daughter-in-law ("In the Ravine"). The superfluous man who had dominated nineteenth-century literature is now joined by the superfluous woman. Both are well-educated, upper-class creatures whose sense of remoteness from society deprives them of any meaningful role in it. Bored with their comfortable lives, yet incapable of working with dirty peasants or teaching children in stifling cabins, they flee into marriages that they expect to cure them of restiveness.

Chekhov's language is clear and precise, usually understating his theme, a quality that is even more apparent in his plays. The dramas are more psychological studies than stories. Like the short stories, they are almost without plot and action. Most of them record the lives of an inert, stagnant gentry incapable of rousing itself to activity. Uncle Vanya, in the play of the same name, slaves away at managing an estate for a brother-in-law whom he cannot respect. *The Three Sisters* all speak of leaving the dull country life and going to Moscow where they could work, but a sense develops that they will never get there. The hero of *The Sea Gull* commits suicide, after his love has an affair with another man.

Chekhov's art is objective—he does not preach or take sides. Yet, occasionally, mixed with the mood of fatalism, futility, and boredom, there are hints of better times to come. The lovers in "The Lady with the Dog" conclude that "it seemed as though in a little while the solution would be found, and then a new and glorious life would begin; and it was clear to both of them that the end was still far off, and that what was to be most complicated and difficult for them was only just beginning."[34]

It is because of these occasional optimistic moments that Soviet Russians have read into Chekhov's works an anticipation of the Revolution of 1917 and the wonderful world that was to follow upon it.

Personally, Dr. Chekhov was the antithesis of the characters he portrayed. He was jovial and witty, deeply involved in his literary work and in doctoring the peasants who lived around his farm outside of Moscow. Though not politically active, he was a man who acted out his convictions. He spent much time, money, and energy to improve the rural educational system. He designed and financed schoolhouses, supplied his hometown library with books and, de-

34. Avrahm Yarmolinsky, ed., *The Portable Chekhov* (New York: Viking Press, 1947), p. 433.

spite ill health, worked as a census taker in 1897. In 1900 he journeyed to the most easterly domains of the Russian empire, on the
island of Sakhalin, to examine the conditions in a penal colony there.
In 1902, when Czar Nicholas II refused to sanction the election of
Maxim Gorky to the Academy of Sciences' literature section, Chekhov and Korolenko were the only two writers who resigned in protest. This episode of the czar interjecting himself in the purely artistic and literary affairs of the academy was to be repeated several
times in the twentieth century when the Soviet government did not
sanction the awarding of the Nobel prize to Pasternak and Solzhenitsyn.

Long ill with tuberculosis, Chekhov refused to follow the calm and
quiet regimen that might have cured him. He died at the age of
forty-four.

Maxim Gorky (1868–1936), the other favorite of the Moscow Art
Theater, also rose to fame as a short-story writer. He, too, suffered
from tuberculosis, but in other respects his career was quite different from Chekhov's.

Maxim Gorky and Leo Tol-
stoy in 1900. *The Bettmann
Archive*

Born Alexis Peshkov, the son of an upholsterer, he later took his pen name from his father's first name, Maxim, and from the Russian word for bitter, *gorky,* to symbolize his impoverished childhood. He wrote mostly about the urban working class and came to be beloved by Soviet Russians as the father of working-class literature and socialist realism.

The revolutionary period in which Gorky grew up, and his own misery in youth made him a socialist in politics and literature. He had only five months of formal schooling, but many years of experiences working and wandering around Russia as a ragpicker, shoemaker's apprentice, gardener, servant, night watchman, hobo, docker, and baker.

He got his first secure job as a journalist in 1893 in his home town. From then on he began to publish stories based on the lower-class people he had met in his wanderings. They were to make him the most popular Russian writer after Tolstoy. In 1898, when a two-volume edition of his stories was published, Gorky attained instantaneous fame. Crowds mobbed him when he appeared on the streets and young people imitated his down-to-earth dress—a white peasant blouse, boots, and walking stick.

His writings opened a whole new perspective on Russian society. The nobility of Tolstoy, the middle-class merchants of Ostrovsky, the gentry and peasants of Chekhov were now joined by the downtrodden working class of Gorky. His plays, particularly *The Lower Depths,* revealed the misery of those who failed in the economic battles for survival. Inspired by his own triumph over the hardships of life, Gorky infused his characters with hope and determination that they, too, would rise up from the lower depths. True to his socialist convictions, Gorky blamed evil not on life itself, like Dostoevsky, but on specific political and material conditions.

His literary and political interests run clearly together in *Mother,* a novel based on the life of a worker, who gets involved in revolutionary activities and ends up in prison, and his mother. The book was the first public picture of the Russian socialist movement and it opposed Chekhov's superfluous, passive man with a new kind of hero, dedicated to a cause and determined to fight for it.

Gorky himself was a "hero of our times." In 1901 he was arrested and imprisoned with other Social Democrats. His tubercular condiiton led to an early release and he went to a Black Sea resort where he met Tolstoy and Chekhov. He was arrested five years later for participating in the Revolution of 1905. He was again imprisoned, but his tuberculosis revived and he was released after much pressure from prominent men throughout Europe.

In 1906 Gorky went to the United States to seek funds for revolutionaries. His tour, like one made a few years later by the Russian composer Scriabin, was a disaster. Both men traveled with their mistresses and found that the American public was affronted by such behavior. Banquets in Gorky's honor were cancelled when this aspect of his personal life was revealed. He returned to Europe and settled in Italy.

But he could not stay away from home and returned to Russia shortly before the start of World War I. He lived through the revolutionary years, deeply committed to the revolution, though critical of its violent methods. He left the Soviet Union in 1921 and finally returned in 1928, having at last made peace with his doubts about the ways in which the new Russia was being led and organized.

The story of artistic perseverance against economic and social obstacles was repeated in the life of Feodor Chaliapin (1873–1938), the world-famous opera basso. Though they did not meet until later, Gorky and Chaliapin had grown up in Nizhni Novgorod (now Gorky) on the Volga River and, in fact, had worked on the same street as apprentices, one to a baker and the other to a shoemaker. Both labored on the river's docks and traveled to Tiflis (now Tbilisi), where they found creative inspiration and help—Gorky publishing his first story and Chaliapin receiving his first singing lessons. Though he became a great opera star at the imperial theaters, Chaliapin left Russia in 1921 for stardom in exile. He and Gorky were friends throughout their adult lives and, while in Italy, Gorky wrote Chaliapin's biography.

It is not unnatural that the great men of any era should know and commune with one another. Gorky was also a great friend of Tolstoy and Chekhov. The relationship among these three, although periodically spiced by exchanges of sharp criticism, was one of deep friendship and even hero worship. Yet the friendship was never allowed to interfere with the evaluation of a colleague's work; indeed, honest appraisal was its highest expression.

Feodor Chaliapin
as Boris Godunov.
The Bettmann Archive

In a letter to Gorky that praised his "genuine, immense talent," Chekhov did not shrink from discussing the younger writer's shortcomings: "I'll begin by saying that in my opinion you have no restraint. You are like a spectator in a theater who expresses his rapture so unreservedly that he prevents himself and others from hearing. This lack of restraint is especially felt in descriptions of nature with which you interrupt your dialogues; when one reads these descriptions one would like them to be more compact, shorter, let us say two or three lines. The frequent reference to voluptuousness, whispering, velvet softness, and so forth, color these descriptions with a certain rhetorical quality and monotony and they chill the reader, almost fatigue him. This lack of restraint is also felt in your descriptions of women. . . ."[35]

Although he was uncommonly famous and successful, Chekhov's life resembled that of other writers. He forged friendships with other artists. He conducted an active correspondence with them on

35. Simmons, *Chekhov*, pp. 439–40.

the art and issues of the day. He struggled against censorship. And he fought commercial battles with rapacious publishing houses.

He also found himself besieged with requests for reviews from beginning writers. Finding it difficult to refuse them, he spent many hours helping a struggling author—hours that might have been better spent on his own writing. The burden was compounded by the social customs of the day, especially the continuous and open receptions at which guests who dropped by for tea might stay the day or, in the country, even a week. Stanislavsky, the actor-director, recorded Chekhov's occasional impatience with these fledgling authors: "Now, listen, tell him that I don't know him and I never studied with him at school," he remembered Chekhov saying. "I know he has a manuscript in his pocket. He'll remain for dinner and read it. This is really impossible."[36] Hospitality was never denied, however, to relatives and friends and Chekhov thirsted for their companionship in the later stages of his illness.

Another custom of the day among the literati was the reading to colleagues of new works. When Chekhov visited Tolstoy in 1895, he heard the latter's aide read aloud from the first draft of the novel, *Resurrection*. Chekhov himself informally tried out his play *The Sea Gull* on a group of friends. The soirées of other artists, who regularly expected guests on Tuesdays or Wednesdays, were welcome opportunities for the exchange of experiences and ideas. They also were the means for introducing aspiring artists to the great talents of the day.

Chekhov's time for serious writing was diminished further by his vast correspondence with friends, relatives, lovers, and colleagues. Despite the existence of the telephone and telegraph, much of the upper-class life in the late nineteenth century was fortunately conducted through and recorded in letters.

Prominent writers were also pressed constantly for financial aid by indigent artists and for political help by revolutionary students. Though Chekhov often gave advice and money, he never participated actively in political affairs, as did Gorky.

For his own income, Chekhov was dependent on the fees paid for his stories by magazines and publishers and on the royalties from

36. *Ibid.,* p. 471.

the production of his plays. He always worried about his income and never attained the financial security and attitude toward money that is evident even among writers of lesser stature in the Soviet Union today. Chekhov often made what friends thought were unprofitable arrangements with publishers for the sale of his works. But he found compensation in the freedom to travel where he liked and to buy land, such as several properties in Yalta—privileges that are not available to Soviet authors today.

Chekhov abhorred one aspect of artistic life in Russia—the special events scheduled to honor an important date in an artist's life, such as his birthday or the twenty-fifth anniversary of his creative work, or a benefit performance to finance the retirement of an actor or ballet dancer.

Shortly before he died Chekhov was himself honored in this way on the night of the premiere of his play, *The Cherry Orchard*. He was forced to stand, weak, pale, coughing from tuberculosis, while long speeches by representatives of newspapers, literary societies, and theaters celebrated his talent.

Probably seated in that first-night audience were the government censors who frequently came to make sure that the work was being performed as approved. Chekhov found the censorship exasperating, for he was often forced to cut out of his stories some realistic details of life in Russia or to alter statements that might be construed as slurs against the state or Russian institutions. Although the czarist censor rejected whole sentences and sections of writing, it was usually still possible to salvage something of the original drafts. Later, under the Soviets, entire works would be doomed to dark drawers, never to be published, or they were published in such small editions that it was predictably impossible to satisfy the public demand. Moreover, many writers began to produce work that the government was known to prefer, thus censoring themselves. The censorship that Chekhov suffered was eventually replaced by the even more complete controls of the Soviet period.

The sinking of the Russian fleet during the Russo-Japanese War in 1904 and the bloody revolution and political repression that followed in 1905 spread disillusionment and disenchantment among the Russian intelligentsia: poets, musicians, and painters spent the next decade fleeing from reality and seeking solace in symbolism and religious yearnings for freedom and a better world.

In the theater this mood was revealed in the Moscow Art Theater's productions of foreign plays by Ibsen, Maeterlinck, and Hauptmann, which offered relief from the realism of current Russian drama.

The composer Alexander Scriabin (1872–1915) described the new music as a "fusion of all the arts but not a theatrical one like Wagner's. Art must unite with philosophy and religion in an indivisible whole to form a new Gospel, which will replace the Old Gospel we have outlined. I cherish the dream of creating such a 'mystery.' "[37] Scriabin never wrote his "mystery"—in which he imagined no one would be a spectator but everyone a participant—but he did approach it with his orchestral works *Divine Poem* and *Prometheus*.

Scriabin's religious mysticism found an echo in the poetry of Vyacheslav Ivanov (1866–1949). Ivanov, whose Wednesday evening salons attracted the intellectual and artistic elite of St. Petersburg, also foresaw a union of art and religion through which Russia would reach new heights of development. Aiming to create an atmosphere and an illusion, like the other symbolists, he emphasized words and sounds in his poetry and juxtaposed Church Slavonic expressions, foreign words, and mythological names. Ivanov believed in the continuity of Russian culture, from as far back as the Scythians, who had lived in southern Russia in the fourth and fifth centuries B.C. and whose gold animal jewelry, uncovered in the eighteenth and nineteenth centuries, is treasured by Russian nationalists. Ivanov's messianic hopes for Russia are similar to those of Alexander Herzen who imagined Russia leading an all-socialist world. The Russians have always been obsessed with this urge to reform and change themselves and then to surge forward to a universal leadership. They have perceived such a path in socialism, in religion, in the adoption of Western ways.

The theme of a new era also pervades the poetry of Andrei Bely (1880–1934). A poet and novelist, Bely's main stylistic interest was in the music and rhythms of his poetic "word symphonies." Bely described the Russian Revolution of 1917 as Russia's crucifixion for

37. Calvocaressi and Abraham, *op. cit.*, pp. 472–73.

the sins of the world and predicted that a new spirit, a new Christ, would rise as a result.

At the end of his famous poem, "The Twelve," Alexander Blok (1880–1921), the greatest of the symbolist poets, has Christ appear as the leader of twelve pro-Bolshevik soldiers who have been plundering and murdering as they march through the streets of St. Petersburg. The twelve soldiers signify the twelve apostles of Jesus and the poem, written in 1918, suggests that a new and better world will arise and justify the horror of the moment. Blok could not anticipate that the Russian Bolsheviks would make Lenin their Christ and communism their faith.

Blok was born into a highly intellectual environment. His father was a professor of law; his mother, the daughter of the rector of the University of St. Petersburg. He grew up in an atmosphere of books, music, and art—in a sense the final flowering of the intellectual elite before the cataclysms of war and revolution destroyed the old styles of life. Blok's marriage to the daughter of the famous chemist Mendeleyev was a love match and his early poems are dedicated to his wife's beauty and to eternal love. But the beauty of life and poetry were soon shattered by the realities of life. Overwhelmed and wearied by events after 1905, Blok took to carousing and extramarital love affairs. He persisted in a kind of self-destruction to divert his mind from the depressing events around him.

Yet in his lyrical poems he clings to the glory of Russia and to faith in her future, often comparing Russia to a fickle woman. Blok welcomed the Revolution of 1917 as a turning point in Russian history, but died disappointed by its results four years later.

For all their religious and allegorical allusions, the symbolists were not "artists for art's sake" but rather poets with a deep commitment to the social and civic function of the artist.

The same melancholy appeared in the painting of the period. Derived from the religious spiritualism of Vrubel and Vasnetsov and recalling medieval iconography, the works of Natalia Goncharova (1881–1962), Michael Larionov (1881–1964), and Marc Chagall (1889–) revived a simple, almost primitive style that turned its back on reality.

The new art no longer had a message for people. It was a private search for truth by the artists that turned their attentions to the nature of form and color, as in the work of Malevich and Kandinsky, or the representation of dreams, as in the canvases of Chagall. Kazimir Malevich (1878–1935) defined his geometric forms as suprematism, the supreme essence of reality.

Many of the painters of this period came from poor families. But they focused on their art, not their poverty, and were soon to be denounced by the new Soviet government of workers and peasants as decadent "formalists" with nothing to offer the Russian people.

4. Moscow: The Frozen North

$\mathbf{T}$HE second Moscow period coincides with the establishment of Communist rule in Russia.[1]

Two revolutions in 1917 brought about the transformation. The first, in March, destroyed the autocracy of the czars and established a republic, headed by Alexander Kerensky. But his weak leadership and refusal to quit World War I emboldened Lenin, the Bolshevik[2] leader, to return from exile with the help of the Germans so that he could undermine the war effort and stage a second revolution. The Bolsheviks overthrew the parliamentary democracy in November and seized power in the name of the people. Fear of being overrun by the still warring Germans caused them to move Russia's capital from St. Petersburg back to the Kremlin in Moscow.

1. Communism has come to mean the kind of government existing in the Soviet Union but it is also the last stage in Karl Marx's theory, the stage at which each person will receive payment not according to his work, but according to his needs. The Russians acknowledge that they have not yet reached this stage.

2. The name Bolshevik party was used until March 1918, when the party adopted a new name—All-Russian Communist (Bolshevik) Party. The term Bolshevik was later omitted.

From his offices in the Kremlin Lenin issued the directives that turned Russia into the Union of Soviet Socialist Republics. Eventually the czars' double-headed eagles on Kremlin towers were replaced by glowing symbols of Communist power—red, five-pointed stars.

Beside the stone and stucco of St. Petersburg, the Moscow of 1918 looked like an antiquated city of wooden huts and narrow streets. For years the two cities had been cultural and social rivals—with Moscow looked down upon as a provincial village, unworthy of the attentions of the northern capital.

Curiously enough, however, Moscow did rival St. Petersburg in the late 1800s as a place of cultural innovation and experiment. St. Petersburg, which sometimes appeared inflexible and conventional to the artists, seemed to suffer from the very presence of the government and its bureaucracy. When the capital shifted again to Moscow, it was St. Petersburg, now called Leningrad,[3] that became the source of innovation, and it remains so to this day, probably for the same reason.

The Moscow years—1917 to the present—have created many different artistic environments, depending on the political currents of the moment. That political ideology should determine the creative production of the country is ironic because the Soviets, preaching Marxism, had insisted that economic conditions really governed the moral and artistic values of a society. Capitalism, they say, breeds bourgeois people who are interested only in material things (houses, cars, refrigerators) and cultural decadence (jazz, modern art, abstract writing). Change capitalism to socialism (or communism), they add, and there emerges a New Soviet Man, freed from economic "exploitation" and from his acquisitive instincts, a selfless human being concerned only with the needs of the whole society.

But political ideology has very much shaped the Soviet cultural scene. Alternately, the Soviet leaders have given artists freedom, shackled them, destroyed them, then revived them again only to purge their ranks and to rekindle fear. To survive, the artist has had to live literally as a political weathervane, watching the prevailing

3. Early in World War I the capital's German-sounding name was changed to Petrograd. After Lenin died, in 1924, it was renamed in his honor.

wind before he chooses themes for his books and paintings or roles for his characters. Through the years of Soviet power, different artists have dealt differently with this problem of survival. Some have developed very precise instincts and twirl in the slightest breeze, producing as best they can whatever they think is wanted. Others defied the Communist party's prescriptions and some of these were destroyed; they were murdered, driven to suicide, sent to labor camps, or denied the right to work. Still others chose to be "silent," not to write or exhibit publicly but to subsist by doing safe things, like translations from the classics. The path followed by each artist seems to be determined by a combination of talent, character, ambition, and circumstance.

1917–1921: Revolution for All

In their ardor after the revolution the Bolsheviks introduced some of their most radical policies. They expected that the peasants, in a surge of brotherly feeling, would gladly feed the urban working class. The peasants, however, refused once they had what they wanted—land. Unexpectedly, there ensued a chaotic and disastrous period called War Communism, in which Russians were at war among themselves, white royalists against red-Bolsheviks—with foreigners fighting on the side of the whites. Famine was widespread and millions died, fighting or starving.

Artists could hardly escape the dangers and burdens of that cold and chaotic time. The hardship was offset only by diversion. To keep warm, people huddled in heated movie houses. Before the showing of each film, dancers or actors performed. The significance of these performances lay not in the entertainment itself, but in the fact that, for the first time, ordinary people could watch performances previously reserved only for the upper classes. The same was true in theaters. Galina Ulanova, the prima ballerina, has recalled that, "The ballet was really a new world to the workers and soldiers who filled the silver-blue halls of the theaters. This theater [the Marinsky] was a vivid example in itself. Formerly it belonged to the court, to the czar's family; and now it belonged to the people and was fully at their disposal. . . . Despite the cold and hunger in Petrograd it opened every evening. This was the place where there was electricity, and the breaths of the audience warmed the hall. Something lovely kept living here, something the people had never seen."[4] Besides performing in cinemas, factories, and village halls, actors were drafted to entertain the Red Army.

The excitement of bringing art to the masses infected other areas too. Inspired by a revolution that promised new economic and social relationships, the artists set out to create a revolutionary art for the new society. They debated the form that this new art should take. Should it be an art incorporating all the people and all the arts in massive theatrical performances? Should it be a totally new proletarian art and blot out the bourgeois, classical heritage of the previous century? Should the new art be produced by only the newly empowered proletariat or could revolutionary sympathizers also contribute? Should the graphic arts be socially useful and functional, rather than merely decorative?

All these questions, however, were eventually subordinated to the Communist party's conception of art, or at least resolved by the party's choice of answers.

Basically, the leaders of the party believed that all art—writing, painting, music, theater—was a tool to be used in educating the masses to accept and serve the new government and its theories. Soon after it seized power, the party placed all theaters under the jurisdiction of the Commissariat of Education. Stripped of their imperial eagles, the theaters passed in 1919 from government supervision to government ownership.

Confronted by artists of many different schools and styles, the government did not at first attempt to regulate the forms of art. But even in these early years, it insisted that the content was to be consistent with official party policy. Though Lenin himself admitted that he did not understand the more advanced artistic forms, such as the poetry of the symbolists, he left them free to create for a time. He almost had no choice, for some of his most idealistic supporters, Blok and Bely, were among them. Revolutionary and progressive in their art before the revolution, they now saw an opportunity for even

---

4. Anna Ilupina, *Ballerina: The Life and Work of Galina Ulanova* (Philadelphia: Provident Pub. Co., 1965), pp. 22–23.

greater aesthetic freedom and experimentation. Eventually though, the innovative spirit they offered the new government was to be destroyed, because the need for conformity conflicted with the artists' need for freedom of style and content.

Despite all the confusion about policy and philosophy, these first years after the revolution were to be the most exciting and imaginative in Soviet history. Painters like Kandinsky and Chagall, like so many other artists who had been working abroad, had hurried home in 1914 to await the end of the war, and now were busily at work.

Immediately after the revolution, and under the guidance of Anatoly Lunacharsky, the commissar of education, the artists set up museums throughout the country, even in Siberia. To support themselves, now that the usual middle-class and upper-class patrons were dead, imprisoned, or in exile, the artists sold their pictures to the government for the new museums. Like their nineteenth-century antecedents, the Wanderers, they were bringing art to the people. The basic difference between the two movements was that while the Wanderers tried to awaken the people's sensibility with socio-critical art in a realistic style, most of the twentieth-century artists worked in the most modern styles. Their sophisticated sculptures and geometric paintings must have appeared incomprehensible to peasants raised on religious icons and simple woodcuts. The transfer of this urban art to the hinterlands demonstrated the great gap that existed between the educated elite and the untrained peasantry. This gap explains, in part, the government's eventual demand for a more realistic and representational art that anyone could "understand."

The museum collections were greatly enhanced by the government's seizure of private art collections from princes and merchants. In the name of the people, the French Impressionist collections of the merchants Shchukin and Morozov passed into the national treasure. They can be viewed today in Moscow's Pushkin Museum, but the Russian canvases of that period, by Kandinsky, Malevich, and Chagall, languish in the basement storerooms of the Tretyakov Gallery, valued commercially, but unacceptable ideologically.

Instruction in the arts also flourished as hundreds of new schools of painting, writing, and theater were filled with applicants. All applicants were accepted, despite the great difficulties this created for the instructors.

Artists taught in other ways, too. Painters and poets were employed for social propaganda: they designed posters and invented slogans to teach people everything from the rudiments of hygiene to better ways of chicken raising. Literacy was encouraged in order to expand the reading and viewing audiences.

Marc Chagall set up an art school in his native town of Vitebsk and organized street processions and poster-painting workshops. His paintings, suffused with color, were lyrical and rich in symbols, using real objects in an unreal manner. His people floated over roofs and men's faces were colored green. Chagall once said to Lunacharsky, "Above all, don't ask me why I painted blue or green and why a calf is visible in the cow's belly, etc. Anyway, let Marx, if he's so wise, come to life and explain it to you."[5]

But this self-confidence was soon shaken. His colleague, Malevich, came to Vitebsk, criticized Chagall as old-fashioned, mobilized faculty and students against him, and replaced him as director. Chagall returned to Moscow, where he managed to find work painting the foyer of the Jewish theater, designing sets, and teaching in a children's school.

Vasily Kandinsky (1866–1944) also tried to help in the administration of art. He was a member of the fine arts division of the Commissariat of Education; a professor at the Art School of the Government Art Workshops; and the founder, in 1919, of the Museum for Pictorial Culture and, in 1921, of the Academy of Aesthetics. As chief of the government purchasing commission for art, he helped establish twenty-two new museums, some in far flung cities such as Perm, Tobolsk, and Ekaterinburg (now Sverdlovsk).

Kandinsky's own paintings were a mixture of vibrant colors and both free and precise shapes, the whole effect portraying no real objects of any kind. He did not believe in depicting the real world on canvas—and even his round soft shapes eventually gave way to the hard lines of geometric forms.

The artists, and not just the Communist party functionaries, battled for power in this period. Their weapons were different aesthetic theories. Vladimir Tatlin (1885–1956), one of the more radical among them, wanted artists to be men of reason, producing work for

5. Marc Chagall, *My Life* (New York. Orion Press, 1960), p. 138.

Improvisation No. 27, a painting by Vasily Kandinsky. *The Metropolitan Museum of Art, the Alfred Stieglitz Collection, 1949*

a social purpose. He named his theory constructivism. Kandinsky, on the other hand, believed that art was psychic and intuitive, not meant for practical purposes. Malevich sided with him against the new utilitarian art. They believed that "art is inevitably, by its very nature, useless, superfluous. . . . In becoming useful, art ceases to exist. . . . The artist ceases to provide the source for new design."[6]

But Tatlin's constructivism suited the time. As its name suggested, constructivist art was to be used to build the new society and to exemplify a spirit of production.

Artists like Lyubov Popova and V. E. Stepanova actually moved to factories and designed fabrics. Others designed furniture and household objects. Because work and workers were now being glorified as the ruling class, artists devoted themselves to making all aspects of factory life aesthetically pleasing, from the workers' clothing to the machinery and the factory buildings themselves.

Unlike the nineteenth-century Wanderers and others who tried to bring art to the people, the constructivists believed that art could

6. Camilla Gray, *The Great Experiment—Russian Art 1863–1922* (New York: Harry Abrams, 1962), p. 243.

not be a passive experience but had to be made directly relevant to life. Their slogan was "Art into life," and their idol was the machine. They believed that the "machine as the source of power in the modern world would release man from labor,"[7] transforming the object made by the machine into art. The artist would assume the functions of the engineer and would learn to supervise the mechanical production of the "object." This branch of constructivism was called "laboratory art" and reflected a strong technical bias. Its critics, who believed in pure art, feared the artist was being reduced to a mere craftsman.

On canvas, constructivism led to the creation of three-dimensional "collages" made of workingman's materials such as coal, glass, paper, wood, and metal. Constructivism found a function, too, in the theater work of Vsevolod Meyerhold and Alexander Tairov. Simple cubes replaced cumbersome chairs so as not to distract the audience, it was said, from an understanding of the play itself. Such scenic design was an obvious reaction to the ideas of Stanislavsky, Meyerhold's former teacher, who had championed the most literal presentation of the natural world.

Constructivism won out over the pure art of Chagall and Kandinsky in the artists' organization sponsored by the government. Discouraged by the hardships of life, the resistance to their ideas, personal rivalries, and intramural disputes, the two artists left again in the early 1920s for France and Germany.

In poetry, too, constructivism found its outlet, largely in the bombastic writings of Vladimir Mayakovsky (1893–1930). Although he was first trained as a painter, Mayakovsky's talents were realized in poetry, in a movement known as futurism. With Boris Pasternak and others, he believed in a break with the classical past and sought new ground for poetic word combinations. As the group declared in a manifesto in 1923: "We refuse to see any distinction between poetry, prose, and speech. We recognize only one medium—the word—and we are using it in our immediate work. We are working for a phonetic organization of the language, for polyphony of rhythm, for the

---

7. *Ibid.*, p. 244.

Constructivism in architecture: a
working people's club in Moscow,
built in 1930. *Tass from Sovfoto*

Vladimir Mayakovsky.
Novosti from Sovfoto

simplification of verbal construction, for the invention of new thematic devices."[8]

To achieve the fusion of poetry and prose and of art and reality, Mayakovsky proposed to write columns of poetry in newspapers. His every effort was to unify art and life, to enlist art in the service of society. His enthusiasm for the Revolution of 1917 was unbounded because it seemed to him to open vistas of creative freedom.

Mayakovsky lived as he preached—flamboyantly. His yellow blazer jacket, often with a carrot or radish in its buttonhole, was meant to challenge conventional attitudes toward proper attire. And his imagery was as bold as his manner: Woodrow Wilson's silk hat was as high as the Eiffel Tower; Chicago had twelve thousand streets.[9] Unlike poetry that was meant to be read in boudoirs, Mayakovsky's was meant to be spoken, shouted, proclaimed in the streets. In his earnest devotion to the Communist cause (though never a Bolshevik himself), Mayakovsky was a most public man. He worked throughout the early years of the revolution as a propagandist, churning out slogans for party campaigns and jingles for government posters. He served also as the editor of *LEF*, the magazine of the futurist movement.

Although the futurists wanted a break with the past, they never denied the past. That was the aim of another new cultural movement of the time, the Proletarian Cultural Educational Organizations (Proletcult), headed by Alexander Bogdanov (1873–1928). Bogdanov sought a proletarian art that owed nothing whatever to Russian history. Adhering to Marx's theory that art was a product of the social system, he believed that since the proletarians were now in power they should have their own class art. To attain this goal he organized state-supported workshops through which he attempted to train the participants in writing techniques. Considering that most of them were people of working-class and peasant origin, with little formal schooling and little knowledge of the past, his approach had some practical value. But the work his proletarian writers produced was negligible and Lenin himself declared in 1920 that "Proletarian culture must be a legitimate development of all the re-

8. Marc Slonim, *Soviet Russian Literature: Writers and Problems 1917–1967* (New York: Oxford University Press, 1967), p. 22.

9. *Ibid.*, p. 26.

serves of knowledge that mankind has accumulated under the pressure of capitalist society, or landlord society, or bureaucrat society."[10] While Proletcult failed as an instrument of artistic mass production, it helped elevate the self-esteem of the proletarian worker. Artists without a proletarian origin were eventually looked down upon and regarded as suspect, and even Mayakovsky felt the scorn of a succeeding generation of proletarians because he had not joined the Communist party.

The audacity of the newly esteemed proletarian class was depicted by Mikhail Zoshchenko in his story "The Westinghouse Brake" in 1926. A drunk, threatened by fellow train passengers with being reported to the police, retorts: "Don't you touch my self-esteem. They can't put me in the clink because of my origin. No matter what I do, I'll get lenient treatment. Because I am a hereditary peasant and proletarian."[11]

The theatrical world also seethed with innovation. In one of those marvelous combinations of talent, which reveal the value of interacting disciplines, Mayakovsky, Meyerhold, and Malevich teamed up in 1918 to produce *Mystery Bouffe*. This propaganda play by Mayakovsky was a pageant, parodying the biblical story of Noah's ark. It showed an "unclean" proletariat vanquishing its "clean" exploiters. Vsevolod Meyerhold, who had broken with Stanislavsky's realism, directed the actors as if they were poster figures. Kazimir Malevich, the suprematist artist, created backdrops using geometric forms and constructions, rather than real props.

This auspicious beginning in joint ventures did not continue for long. Mayakovsky committed suicide in 1930; Malevich's geometric art was soon eclipsed by the more acceptable realist art; and Meyerhold's theater was forced to close in the 1930s.

One of the most elaborate experiments, based on the mass participation festivals of the French Revolution, was organized by the director Nikolai Yevreinov (1879–1953) for the third anniversary of the revolution in Petrograd. Reenacting the storming of the Winter Palace, Evreinov commanded a cast of eight thousand, an orchestra of five hundred, and a real blast of gunfire from the battleship *Aurora*.

---

10. *Ibid.*, p. 35.
11. F. D. Reeve, ed., *Great Soviet Short Stories* (New York: Dell, 1962), p. 451.

These spectacles bespoke the thesis that art should no longer be an elite enterprise for a small group of consumers, but edification for all people. Involvement of "all the people" in such productions was supposed to create a sense of brotherhood and comaraderie.

Though these extravaganzas did not become commonplace, the idea of mass participation survives to this day in the celebration of the Soviet Union's two most important public holidays, May Day and November 7. The parades on these days are massive; military troops, sportsmen, and ordinary citizens marching for hours past only a few political leaders and honored spectators.

Yevreinov's direction of the huge spectacle in 1920 brought him not money, which had lost most of its value, but scarce goods. He received a fox fur coat and each of his assistants was paid a dozen eggs and a half pound of tobacco. Similarly, actors were encouraged to join the numerous road companies for "salaries" of bread, lard, and butter.

The ballerina Tamara Karsavina has recorded how the commander-in-chief of the Moscow garrison visited her after one performance and offered not the customary bouquet of flowers, but a bag of flour.

For many artists, especially theatrical and ballet personalities who had been well rewarded by the imperial court, the transition to the new economic and cultural situation was overwhelming. They had been hurled from the pampered days of maids, carriages, and regular performance schedules into a period of aggressive egalitarianism, no more servants, greetings of "comrade" instead of "sir" or "madam," hectic schedules, and impromptu performances in drafty workingmens' clubs.

But famine, frost, typhoid fever, and breadlines were not the only hardships. Censorship, disciplinary measures for anti-revolutionary thoughts, control of printing presses and paper mills restricted the writer as writer. The real problem for all artists was creative freedom. Yevgeni Zamyatin(1884–1937), a writer and shrewd observer of the era, wrote as early as 1921: "Russian writers are accustomed to going hungry. The main reason for their silence lies neither in the lack of bread nor in the lack of paper; the reason is far weightier, far tougher, far more ironclad. It is that true literature can exist only where it is created, not by diligent, reliable officials, but by madmen, hermits, heretics, dreamers, rebels, and skeptics. And when a writer must be prudent, sensible, and rigidly orthodox, when he must be useful at the present moment, when he cannot lash out at everyone like Swift, or smile at everything like Anatole France, then there is no bronze literature,[12] then there is only a flimsy paper literature, a newspaper literature, which is read today and used for wrapping soap tomorrow."[13]

Zamyatin described his fears for the new Communist society in 1920 in a political fantasy, *We*. He imagined a glassed-over city with a perfect climate in which the inhabitants are assigned numerals. All thought is controlled by the Benefactor and technological devices pick up every sound that is uttered. One of the citizens, D-503, dares to think for himself and falls in love. He is cured of his crime in an operation which causes him to betray all other Enemies of Happiness. *We* was published in English in 1924 and probably influenced George Orwell's *1984*, a similar satire on a police state.

The outspoken Zamyatin became one of the earliest victims of the repression he diagnosed. In 1931 he petitioned Stalin for permission to leave the Soviet Union and he died in exile.

Zamyatin's thoughts were echoed by Maxim Gorky. The pre-revolutionary writer, himself not a Bolshevik, vigorously supported the aims of the revolution but found himself recoiling in horror from its repressive and vengeful methods. He wrote, "Lenin and Trotsky have become infected by the bacillus of power; they show a disgraceful attitude toward the freedoms of speech and of person and toward all democratic rights."[14]

Gorky, like many other artists of the revolutionary period, spent the early years shuttling in and out of exile. Ballet dancers, musicians, and painters, whose skills and therefore whose livelihoods were not dependent on knowledge of a foreign language, adjusted fairly well to life abroad. But the writers found they could live neither in their homeland nor away from it. So they had to choose be-

12. This is an allusion to the literature of the nineteenth century, commonly known as the Golden Age, and to literature of the early twentieth century, the Silver Age. Presumably the Soviet era would have been known as the Bronze Age.

13. Vera Alexandrova, *A History of Soviet Literature: 1917–1964. From Gorky to Solzhenitsyn* (Garden City, N.Y.: Doubleday, 1963) p. xiii.

14. Marc Slonim, *From Chekhov to the Revolution: Russian Literature 1900–1917* (New York: Oxford University Press, 1962), p. 48.

tween the repression of a single-minded government and the obscurity and discomfort of life in an alien society; some chose one way, some another. For those who had studied or lived abroad in their youth, the transition to a foreign environment was not too difficult; others preferred the security of familiar surroundings.

Though inwardly troubled, Gorky decided eventually to support the revolution. By lending his prestigious name to the Communists, he was rewarded with a degree of influence which he used to help others in trouble. To save hundreds of artists and intellectuals from starvation and death, he created a huge state-supported publishing house, International Literature, and gave them employment.

Gorky eventually settled down in the Soviet Union. He died in 1935, perhaps naturally or perhaps by poison, as suggested in suspect testimony at the purge trials.

1921–1928: Revolution for Some

As the civil war subsided, the victorious Bolsheviks retreated from the hasty imposition of their theories and introduced the New Economic Policy. NEP (1921–1928) was a temporary retreat to capitalism and private—rather than state—ownership of the means of production and distribution. The party relented so as to assuage the wounds of a country that had been at war for seven years.

The economic retreat brought some respite for artists too. Though many supported the ideals of the revolution, few of them were actual party members. The Bolshevik party had always been a small, tightly knit group. Once in power, it adhered to Lenin's principle of limiting membership to preserve the party's effectiveness. Even today's oft-expanded membership of the Communist party represents only 5 percent of the total population.

During NEP the party did not stress conformity in style and artists were free to indulge their revolutionary spirit with all kinds of experimental techniques. Hence the 1920s produced a good deal of ferment. Abstract forms dominated the graphic arts. Technology inspired a new kind of drama. Montages and other novel techniques appeared in films. Writers competed in the proclamation of rival proletarian literatures. The artists of different disciplines joined in theatrical experiments and their verve and daring dazzled the rest of the world.

But the variety of these years was deceptive. It masked a reaction to the avant-garde spirit set off by the revolution.

Suprematists and constructivists began to feel the challenge of those who wished to revive realism in painting. In 1922 an exhibition of the Wanderers—the nineteenth-century painters of social criticism—and their followers won acclaim from the people and the government. Only two years later, as revolutionary enthusiasm declined, the commissar of education, Lunacharsky, announced, "Back to Ostrovsky!" He meant a return to the realistic and tame criticism of social manners that had been popular with Russian dramatists at the end of the nineteenth century.

On the literary front, too, writers were dividing into two main groups: the fellow travelers who sympathized with the revolution but did not commit their work to its cause, and the proletarians who felt the revolution required a class-conscious art devoted to its objectives. The fervor and pressure of the proletarians caused some of the more independent authors to complain of "coercion and boredom and . . . everybody writing in the same way."[15]

One of the casualties of this intramural conflict was Sergei Yesenin (1895–1925), a poet, who committed suicide. The son of a peasant, Yesenin wrote intensely personal poetry rich in earthy images. Like Mayakovsky, he lived in a flamboyant manner which he dramatically demonstrated in a marriage to a woman twice his age, Isadora Duncan, the innovative American ballet dancer. But the exuberance of his life style was perhaps just a cover for the difficulty he found in adapting to the new artistic demands. His suicide symbolized the disillusionment of the artist with the regime and set a family precedent; years later his son was also to find himself opposed to the government's policies.

Lenin's death in 1924 marked the beginning of a harsher period of political repression and conflict. While Lenin was elevated to a kind of sainthood (giving employment to thousands of painters, sculptors, writers, and musicians who were needed to sing his praises), his successor, Stalin, moved toward a new autocracy. He

15. Slonim, *Soviet Russian Literature*, p. 98.

Sergei Yesenin.
Novosti from Sovfoto

eliminated his opponents, in and out of the party, decreed a new ideological orthodoxy, and prepared for a rigorous economic program of forced industrialization and seizure of all privately held farm land.

Abetted by this drift toward "Stalinism," the proletarian groups strove hard to establish their authority over the fellow travelers. Though the party declared in 1925 that "it cannot allow, by decree or proclamation, any legal monopoly of literary production on the part of one group or literary organization, and cannot grant this monopoly to any group—not even to the proletariat group itself," the opposite was in fact occurring.[16]

The music world, too, split into modernists and proletarians. Prominent composers like Rachmaninov, Prokofiev, Medtner, Gretchaninov, and Glazunov moved into exile as the pressures closed in. Lost with them were not just countless compositions but also their training and inspiration of later generations of musicians.

Only one new composer could be said to be partially filling the void. He was Dmitri Shostakovich (1906–), whose First Symphony (1926) was warmly received everywhere. Conforming to the de-

16. *Ibid.*, p. 49.

mand for socialist themes, Shostakovich's next symphonies were named *October* (1927) and *May Day* (1929). Lesser contemporary compositions were also built around revolutionary themes, such as Alexander Mossolov's *Iron Foundry,* Vissarion Shebalin's *Lenin Symphony,* and Reinhold Glière's *The Red Poppy.*

The emphasis on revolutionary themes also brought a recognition of the Soviet Union's multi-national character and a revival of folk songs and folk motifs in opera, ballet, and symphonies. Hardly any of the remaining composers in Russia experimented with dodecaphony, the tone scale that had been developed in Vienna in the early 1900s by Arnold Schoenberg and Carl von Webern and had inspired new musical trends in most other Western countries.

The theater and film worlds were spared political convulsions for a time. Aesthetic differences were heatedly debated, but no one of the directors sought absolute authority over his colleagues. The most interesting theatrical personalities of the period were Vsevelod Meyerhold (1874–1942), Alexander Tairov (1885–1950), and Eugene Vakhtangov (1883–1922).

The point of departure for all three was the work of Stanislavsky. Meyerhold rejected his naturalism and claimed that the theater should not merely duplicate life. He wanted it to add a new dimension to experience—an air of deliberate theatricality. Toward that end, he formulated the theory of biomechanics. Stanislavsky erred, he said, by so concentrating on emotions that his actors did not know how to move. Meyerhold stressed stylized movement, based on reflex actions and pantomime, instead of psychology.

The plays he performed were satirical attacks on the Western world and on both czarist and Soviet Russia. For his biting commentary on old Russia, Meyerhold turned to the Russian classics, such as Griboyedov's *Woe from Wit* and Gogol's *Inspector General.* His assaults on Soviet bureaucracy were through Mayakovsky's two poetic plays, *The Bedbug* and *The Bathhouse,* produced in 1929 and 1930, just before Mayakovsky's suicide.

In *The Bedbug,* Mayakovsky condemned party bureaucrats who took advantage of their power to enrich themselves. *The Bathhouse* was a harangue against a system in which "the obeying of directives, the preparation of circulars, and the implementation of efficiency are executed by having papers lie around for years in a state

A scene from Mayakovsky's play *The Bedbug*, 1929.
Novosti from Sovfoto

of total chaos. For request, complaints, and memoranda, there is a production line."[17]

Diversity came to the theater as if in obedience to Karl Marx's theory of history: that each thesis produces its opposite (antithesis) and then merges with it into a new synthesis. If Stanislavsky's naturalism was the thesis, and Meyerhold's symbolism and mechanization the antithesis, then the synthesis, so thought Alexander Tairov, was the theater of "emotional gesture." Tairov rejected both Stanislavsky's idea that the actor should seek to recreate a character's genuine emotions and Meyerhold's deemphasis of emotion. As he saw it, the actor should create the character out of his own fantasy. In addition Tairov conceived of drama as a musical performance in which the actors' sounds and gestures created melodies and rhythms.

Eugene Vakhtangov was, like Meyerhold, a student of Stanislavsky. He later became director of the First Studio, an offshoot of Stanislavsky's Moscow Art Theater. Although he died young, he made a significant contribution to Soviet theater. He—and not Tairov —was the true synthesizer who combined Meyerhold's theatricality —the idea that the theater must go beyond the limits of ordinary reality—with Stanislavsky's emphasis on the psychological expression of character.

Ironically, Stanislavsky's "real realism," so despised by his revolu-

17. Nikolai Gorchakov, *The Theater in Soviet Russia*, trans. Edgar Lehrman (New York: Columbia University Press, 1957), p. 218.

A scene from Nikolai Pogodin's *The Aristocrats,* produced by Vakhtangov.
Sovfoto

tionary successors, is the only theatrical system encouraged by the
Soviet government. The Moscow Art Theater still performs the
Chekhov masterpieces as Stanislavsky mounted them more than
seventy years ago. But Meyerhold's theater was closed in the 1930s
and he died in the purges of that decade. Tairov's theater was closed
in 1949 and he died soon after. The Vakhtangov Theater continues
to function, but only as an extension of the Stanislavsky system.
Present-day theaters that attempt to be modern in the Meyerhold
tradition often run into trouble with the government and find their
productions abruptly cancelled.

The cultural revolutionaries spawned by the political revolution
found themselves quickly eclipsed by old-fashioned realists who
proved more suitable to the party's propaganda purposes.

The same thing finally happened in films, although not until Sergei
Eisenstein, Dziga Vertov, and Vsevolod Pudovkin had left their im-
press on the infant industry. Lenin had foreseen the power of the
new medium, declaring in 1921 that "the cinema is for us the most
important of all the arts."[18] His commissar of education, Lunacharsky,
deployed it not as an art in itself, but as a reproductive device to
send stage plays around the country.

For a time film makers clung to the assumption that they were
simply a branch of the theater. They, too, repudiated reality for

18. United States Information Agency, *Problems of Communism,* Washington,
D. C.: November/December, 1954, p. 35.

symbolism. But then came Dziga Vertov's new film doctrine of "factography," proposing documentary films to be made by amateur actors, without special scenery, in "factual" settings.

Another innovator, Lev Kuleshov, developed a method of montage filming—cutting and splicing film so as to juxtapose different sequences to achieve the desired effect. The technique was born of necessity; because of a shortage of new film Kuleshov had to make movies by rearranging old film. But it led to much more.

Sergei Eisenstein (1898–1948), a former pupil of Meyerhold's and a theatrical director, synthesized these three concepts—symbolism, factography and montage—to produce in 1925 the internationally acclaimed movie *Potemkin.* It signified the cinema's break with the theater by using natural settings with casts of thousands and by presenting a narrative with several plots and from several points of view. As in the other arts, however, the avant-garde dramatic tendencies of Mayakovsky, Meyerhold, and Eisenstein were challenged by realists. Their leader in films was Vsevolod Pudovkin. Stressing authentic and precise performance, he produced *Mother,* a film version of Maxim Gorky's novel of the same name, *The End of St. Petersburg,* and *Storm over Asia.*

For a time, there were also poetic and lyrical movies, like Alexander Dovzhenko's *Soil,* a classic of the silent era. In this film Dovzhenko glorified the wonders of the machine: he dramatized the reluctance of peasants to accept the new tractors and through skillful cinematography depicted the mechanical transformation of a sheaf of wheat into a loaf of bread. But the realists won out in the party and when they finally clamped down, they established a tighter grip on the mass medium of film than on any other art form.

Hence the decade that began with such grand hopes for the future of Russian culture ended in despair. The end of diversity in the arts paralleled an end of diversity in party and government. Political leaders such as Bukharin, Zinoviev, Kamenev, and Trotsky, who had supported a more lenient approach to the arts and artists, themselves became Stalin's victims.

Mayakovsky, the brash spokesman for a new aesthetic, died a broken man, his hopes for the new Russia crushed by repression and uniformity. He, who had commented so sternly upon the suicide of the poet Sergei Yesenin in 1925, shot himself on April 14,

1930. Two months before he died, he had relented and joined the government-sponsored Russian Association of Proletarian Writers.

A month before his death, still trying to please the authorities, he said, "Although I do not carry a party card, I do not separate myself from the party, and consider myself bound to carry out all decisions of the Bolshevik party." But in his suicide poem, he wrote to the wife of a friend:

> Already past one. You must be in bed.
> Across the night and Milky Way, a silver Oka River
> I am in no hurry and am not going to wake you
> with special telegrams and disturb you;
> As they say, the incident is closed,
> *Love boat smashed against environment;*
> Life and I are quits.
> No need of listing mutual hurts, sorrows and grievances.
> Look how peaceful the world.
> Night has imposed on the sky a starry contribution.
> *At just such hours one rises up and speaks to ages, to*
>   *history, to creation* [italics added][19]

1928–1940: Revolution for None

The dominant influence on a generation of Soviet life and art, starting in 1928, was Stalin, a Georgian Communist who had gradually gained personal control of the party and the country after Lenin's death. He established himself as the arbiter of aesthetics and decreed a new philosophy of art, socialist realism. For political purposes he destroyed every potential source of opposition within the party and among intellectuals by means of the purges of the 1930s. Through what was later called a "cult of personality," he became literally the model for much of the painting and sculpture done in the Soviet Union during his reign. Many were the poems written to, for, and about Stalin. Yevgeni Yevtushenko recounts in *A Precocious Auto-*

19. Alexander Kaun, "Vladimir Mayakovsky, 1894–1930," *American Quarterly on the Soviet Union*, January 1930, p. 21, as quoted in *Problems of Communism* 3, July/August 1954, p. 19.

Glory to the Great Stalin! demonstrates the extent of the personality cult in Russian painting. *Sovfoto*

biography how a poem he wrote for the newspaper *Soviet Sport* about May Day suddenly acquired four new lines when the editor felt compelled to mention Stalin's name before he dared publish it: "I soon had a thorough understanding of the rules: for a poem to go through there had to be a few lines devoted to Stalin. This even began to seem perfectly natural to me. And so, of course, I no longer had to have such verses written for me—I wrote them myself."[20] Stage and screenplays all paid tribute to the Great Leader.

The year 1928 was a turning point in Soviet history. Eleven years after the revolution, four years after Lenin's death, it brought the simultaneous end of the lax economic period, NEP, and the imposition of the first of the five-year plans. There was to be no more fooling around with capitalist compromises. Marxist theory, as defined by Stalin, was to be put into practice.

The prime loser in the ideological battles was Leon Trotsky, commissar of war, and a prominent co-worker of Lenin in the early years of the revolution. Trotsky believed that true communism could be

20. Yevgeni Yevtushenko, *A Precocious Autobiography,* trans. Andrew R. MacAndrew (New York: E. P. Dutton, 1963), p. 68.

achieved only through a worldwide revolution. He argued that the purpose of launching a revolution in Russia had been to create a base of operations to inspire the proletariat, or working classes, of all industrial countries to rise up against capitalism. Stalin, with more realism, decided to concentrate on "building communism in one country." Trotsky was demoted, exiled, then expelled from the Soviet Union, and finally killed by Stalin's agents. His name disappeared from Soviet textbooks and encyclopedias. He was mentioned in Soviet life only as the author of a plot to kill off one of Stalin's favorites in the mid-1930s, an incident that became the pretext for the mass purges that followed.

The first Five-Year Plan decreed the development of heavy industry, the collectivization of agriculture into cooperative, state farms, and the elimination of all "bourgeois" elements.

Artists were also collectivized in 1932. All the once-independent and varied groups of writers formed in the 1920s were disbanded and replaced by one union of writers.

Similar unions were set up for musicians and "artists," a broad term covering graphic artists, decorative artists, sculptors, and architects. The union was given "exclusive control of the facilities for creative work: exhibit halls, studios, working materials and supplies, orders for specific works, etc."[21] The union in turn was controlled by the Commissariat of Culture and the Communist party. All orders for paintings were transmitted through state and party-run organizations. Artists were instructed to paint or write on patriotic themes, such as "Anniversary of the Red Army" or "Workers on a Collective Farm," and their wages were fixed by a union scale. Members regularly had to attend political courses and were expected to "volunteer" their time for state projects, such as the building of the subway.

A new principle of aesthetics was formulated—socialist realism— which the unions were to apply in all creative endeavors. Andrei Zhdanov, a Communist party spokesman and Stalin aide, explained it like this in 1934: "Socialist realism, being the basic method of Soviet literature and criticism, requires from the artists truthful, historically concrete representation of reality in its evolutionary development. Moreover, truth and historical completeness of artistic

21. *Problems of Communism,* May/June 1962, p. 53.

representation must be combined with the task of ideological transformation and education of the working man in the spirit of socialism."[22]

Maxim Gorky, who wrote on proletarian themes even before the
revolution, correctly saw that socialist realism was "purpose" art as
opposed to pure art and that the doctrine confronted artists with an
age-old question. For hundreds of years Christianity had used music,
architecture, and painting to inspire simple people to accept its faith
and to worship its symbols. It was the beauty of the Byzantine
church service that is said to have persuaded Prince Vladimir's emis-
saries to select the Greek Orthodox over every other tenth-century
religion. In the nineteenth century, writers such as Chernyshevsky
and Tolstoy, and painters such as Repin, also acknowledged art as
a social tool that could arouse in people awareness of the problems of
society.

The Communists, too, valued art for its utility in encouraging
people to accept their political philosophy. It was ironic, however,
that this "revolutionary" movement looked back for its models to
the realism of the nineteenth-century Russian classics, rather than
create its own classics, as many artists wished.

Socialist realism required poems, plays, operas, novels, and movies
to deal with contemporary themes, such as collectivization and industrialization, and to have as their heroes people on whom the
Soviet masses could model their own behavior. The "positive hero"
never did anything wrong; he was the irreproachable New Soviet
Man whom the party expected to create with its new classless economic system. Besides being socialist in theme, the culture also was
to be "realistic." It had to educate the masses and therefore be easily
understandable. On the stage a chair had to be represented by a
chair, not by a box; in art, smiling cheerful faces had to be faces, not
distorted abstractions.

Socialist realism had two purposes: to enlist artists as the party's
agents in the indoctrination of the people, and to maintain strict
control on artistic production so that art would serve no hostile
ideology or faction.

22. Marc Slonim, *Russian Theater. From the Empire to the Soviets* (New York:
Collier Books, 1962), p. 332.

Rumanian Peasants' Delegation at the Kharkov Tractor Plant, a painting in the tradition of socialist realism. *Sovfoto*

In practice, however, socialist realism came to mean much more than socialist themes in realistic settings. It meant that writers were not allowed to describe Soviet life as they saw it. They had to omit from their works anything that reflected badly on the accomplishments of the new system and include instead whatever the Communist party wished was true.

In describing characters, the writer could not portray a balanced personality; he was constrained to divide all people into good and bad, right and wrong. Vera Panova was criticized for being "so merciless toward good people that she turns a searchlight on their faults, compelling us repeatedly to change our attitude toward her heroes, and in the end leaving us baffled. Why is she so kind toward bad people that she turns her searchlight on their smallest virtue?"[23]

To be "socialist realist," art had to portray life not as it was but as it would be. The tone of a book or a painting had to be optimistic, showing people enthusiastically building communism. It was not "realism," but this distortion of realism into fantasy that eroded the creative will of many artists.

23. Alexandrova, *op. cit.,* p. 324.

All experimentation in the arts came to an end. Geniuses of the theater and cinema, like Meyerhold and Eisenstein, found their styles severely cramped and had to choose between public criticism and private resignation. Musicians were similarly affected by the newly imposed doctrine. Prokofiev, who had returned to the Soviet Union in 1933 after a fifteen-year absence, at first tried to write down to the people but later said that it was "a mistake to strive for simplification." Some of his serious music was not published but he adapted to the new demands by composing some of his most popular music: the children's story *Peter and the Wolf,* the film orchestral suite *Lieutenant Kije,* the ballet *Romeo and Juliet,* and the scores for the movies *Alexander Nevsky* and *Ivan the Terrible,* both directed by Eisenstein.

But there was no ideological safety in historical themes or in librettos based on Russian classical literature, as the composer Dmitri Shostakovich found out. His opera *Katerina Izmailova,* based on *Lady Macbeth of Mtsensk District,* a tale by the nineteenth-century writer Nikolai Leskov, was acclaimed when it premiered in Leningrad in 1934. When Stalin saw it two years later in Moscow he so disliked it that it was shelved for the next twenty years.

Individualism in writing also ceased. Writers, like Boris Pasternak, one of the futurist poets whose works were esoteric and difficult even for interested Russians to understand, forsook poetry as a livelihood and took up translating Shakespeare's plays. Others "wrote for the drawer," a Russian expression meaning not for immediate publication. And some, like Marina Tsvetaeva, in 1941, took their lives. Many had no choice at all. In the purges of 1936–1938, hundreds of artists were seized, incarcerated, put to work in labor camps, and murdered.

The majority of writers adapted to the new credo. To grasp "socialist reality" they took to the road and visited collective farms, factories, virgin lands, dam sites, lumber camps, and machine tractor stations. The novels and movies that resulted from these expeditions to "get closer to life" usually described an ardent, selfless worker overcoming an evil, anti-Soviet type interested only in self-aggrandizement. They were often devoid of a romantic plot, the ardent worker being too preoccupied with his machines to be interested in a woman. Such literature, no matter how pleasing to party function-aries, failed at the box office and in the bookstores. Yuri Olesha, the short-story writer, explained why at the First Congress of Soviet Writers in 1934.

"While I was thinking about the story of my beggar, our country was building factories. It was the time of the first Five-Year Plan, the very time when the socialist national economy was being created.

"But this was not a subject for me. Certainly, I could have gone out on a construction site, lived in a factory among the workers and described them in an article, or even in a novel. But that was not my theme, the theme in my blood, in my breath. I couldn't handle that subject matter as a true artist. I would have been forced to con-trive, to lie. I wouldn't have had what is known as inspiration. It is difficult for me to conceive the type of a worker, a revolutionary hero. Because I cannot be him.

"It is beyond my strength, beyond my understanding. and this is why I do not write about him."[24]

But the readers of such "industrial" novels also had artistic com-plaints. They didn't want to read about machines; they wanted to read about life, love, and humanity. They sought their entertainment in the works of Alexei N. Tolstoy, Konstantin Fedin, Leonid Leo-nov, and Mikhail Sholkohov who each, in different ways, wrote nov-els that remain in circulation to this day. All except Sholokhov are writers whose literary heritage is clearly pre-revolutionary and who found it difficult to write in the "socialist realist" manner. Alexei N. Tolstoy (1883–1945), a more faithful party-liner, wrote *The Road to Calvary,* a popular trilogy about the intelligentsia against the background of World War I and the revolution. He was also fasci-nated by the figures of Ivan the Terrible and Peter the Great about whom he wrote a play and a novel. Fedin's (1892–) work is perme-ated with the conflict of the intellectual who, in theory, is for revolu-tion but who, in practice, finds it difficult to accept the demands of this particular Russian revolution. Fedin has become active in the politics of the writers' union and was particularly prominent in the decisions taken not to publish the works of Pasternak and Solzheni-

24. Yuri Olesha, *Envy and Other Works* (New York: Doubleday, 1967), pp. 216–17.

tsyn in recent years. Leonov (1899–) has been preoccupied with the psychology of man. His novels are rich in language and reflect the concern with words of the futurists and other writers of the 1920s. Sholokhov's (1905–) powerful novels about the civil war period, *And Quiet Flows the Don,* and about collectivization, *Virgin Soil Upturned,* earned him the respect of Stalin and acclaim throughout the world, as well as financial success.

But nothing written in these years could match the real life drama of the great purges. In December 1934 one of Stalin's associates, Kirov, the party leader of Leningrad, was killed under suspicious circumstances that have led many to wonder whether Stalin himself had ordered his death. Several months before, Stalin had asked the Central Committee of the Communist Party for power to arrest and kill any ideological deviant, even if he were a party member. The central committee denied Stalin that right and Stalin now needed to justify such extraordinary power. The Kirov murder became his justification because in trials that began in 1936 he blamed it on his own former colleagues, Zinoviev, Bukharin, and Trotsky.

At first the trials condemned only political persons involved with the party. Then they reached out to military personnel, then to people who were only acquainted with military people, and eventually to the intellectuals. This ever-widening circle of arrest, trial, and destruction, replete with staged investigations, false accusations, and false confessions, solidified Stalin's authority. By destroying all his former colleagues, those who had differed with him ideologically and all those who might do so, Stalin sought to protect himself and the state against all further challenge.

The terror and fear of those years is well described by Ilya Ehrenburg in his autobiography, *Men, Years—Life.* He recounts how, on returning to Moscow from Spain in December 1936, his daughter and son-in-law informed him of the fearsome situation. "I was very agitated and at every name asked: 'But why him?' Lapin tried to think of explanations: Pilnyak had been to Japan; Tretyakov often met foreign writers; Pavel Vasilev drank and talked too much. Bruno Jasenski was a Pole—all the Polish Communists had been arrested—Artem Vesely had at one time been a member of the *Pereval* (the Pass) literary group; the wife of the painter Shukha-

Ilya Ehrenburg.
Tass from Sovfoto

Isaac Babel.
Sovfoto

yev was acquainted with Gogoberidze's nephew; Charents was too popular in Armenia; Natasha Stolyarov had just come from France. Irina answered my questions each time: 'How can I know? Nobody knows.' Lapin advised me with a rueful smile: 'Don't ask anyone. And if someone starts talking about it, just shut up.'" Other artists, he recalled, like Sergei Prokofiev, were "unhappy, even grim, and said to me: 'Today one must work. Work's the only thing, the only salvation.'" Still others "tried to shut themselves off, seeing only their closest relatives; suspicion, apprehension undermined friendly intercourse. Babel said: 'Today a man talks frankly only with his wife—at night, with the blanket pulled over his head.'"[25]

This was a reference to his friend, the writer Isaac Babel (1894–1941). A Jew, born in Odessa, Babel made his way as a young man to Petrograd where he was befriended by the famed writer Maxim Gorky. In his story, "The Beginning," Babel recounts Gorky's thrilling and prophetic speech to him upon accepting his manuscript for the magazine *Letopis*:

"'There are small nails,' said Gorky, 'and there are large ones, as

25. Ilya Ehrenburg, *Memoirs, 1921–1941*, trans. Tatania Shebunina in collaboration with Yvonne Kapp (Cleveland and New York: World Pub., 1964; London: Macgibbon & Kee, 1963) pp. 420, 424, 425.

large as my finger.' And he raised to my eyes a long, powerful and delicately modeled finger. 'A writer's path is studded with nails, mostly of the large variety. You will have to walk on them barefoot, and you will bleed profusely, more profusely every year. . . . If you are weak, you will be bought and sold, you will be shaken and harassed and put to sleep, and you will wilt away, pretending you are a tree in bloom. . . . But for an honest man, for an honest writer and revolutionary, traveling along this road is a great honor; to which arduous undertaking, my dear sir, I now bless you. . . .' "[26]

Although the party had always treated him well, rewarding his work with an apartment, servants, a car, and a country house, Babel refused to yield to party pressure to write as directed. He was arrested in May 1939, tried by a military tribunal in January 1940, and died in March 1941. He was "rehabilitated" by another military tribunal, in December 1954, in a document that revoked his earlier sentence "on the basis of newly discovered circumstances" and called the case against him "terminated in the absence of elements of a crime."[27]

The major new circumstance was Stalin's death a year before which led to thousands of "rehabilitations." But until that moment the victims, like Babel, were unpersons—nothing was said about them, nothing was published by or about them.

The purges were a relentless and arbitrary scourge, striking the most famous, the innocent, the unsuspecting, maiming with fear even those fortunate enough not to have been physically touched.

Years later the poet Yevgeni Yevtushenko, musing about Vladimir Mayakovsky, asked:

> Would he have glumly stepped aside,
> kept silent,
> > gritting his teeth
> > > from a distance,

26. Alexandrova, *op. cit.*, p. 146.
27. *Isaac Babel, The Lonely Years 1925–1939*, trans. Andrew R. MacAndrew and Max Hayward. Ed. with an Introduction by Nathalie Babel (New York: Farrar, Straus, 1964), p. xxviii.

when somewhere in the night,

          in Black Marias

Bolsheviks were taken for execution?

I don't believe it!

Inflexibly,

        botheringly

he would have risen, flinging

           his prophetic thunder,

Being dead, he has become

        "The best

           and most talented" . . .

alive

  he would have been declared an enemy of the people.[28]

1940–1953: *Reprise*

World War II threatened the destruction of Soviet Russia, but ironically it gave new life to the creative scope of art and artists there. The purges of the intellectuals, the party, and the military were interrupted by the even bloodier purge of Russia by the Nazi Germans—twenty million dead and fourteen million wounded.

The war diverted the government's attention from enemies at home to enemies abroad and it turned the fear and resentment of artists into patriotic fervor and zeal. Writers and poets enlisted in the armed forces as military correspondents. Painters and musicians contributed to the propaganda battles at home.

The literature that ensued was not remarkable, but it was permitted to break with the suffocating demands of socialist realism and to describe the travails of the common citizen and the ordinary soldier. It was freer in spirit and style, and the gripping tales of personal courage made exciting reading for those whose literary fare had been limited to melodramatic tales of party officials uncovering bourgeois agents on collective farms. Lasting literary contributions came from Konstantin Simonov in *Nights and Days,* a novel about the battle of Stalingrad, and Alexander Tvardovsky's poem *Vasily Tyorkin.* The

28. Yevgeni Yevtushenko, *Bratsk Station and Other Poems* (New York: Doubleday, 1967), p. 142.

war itself, for all the hardship and desolation it imposed on the Russian people, engendered "a foreboding of freedom" and the hope that the purges had been but a single and singular event in Soviet history.

But these feelings of optimism and solidarity were soon shattered. In 1946 Andrei Zhdanov, Stalin's agent who, a decade earlier, had launched the campaign to herd artists into professional unions, reappeared on the cultural scene to restore the leash with denunciations and threats of severe punishment. The new purge atmosphere, which condemned some of the great names of Soviet cultural life to creative silence, lasted beyond Zhdanov's own mysterious death in 1948, until the death of Stalin in 1953.

Some blamed Stalin's return to the old ways on paranoia, on his own dark and sick suspicions and fears. But there were more tangible reasons too. The party had to restore its sway over the country —a devastated country whose economic recovery would require decades more of hardship, sacrifice, and discipline. And there was now a foreign threat—or at least a rival—against which the Soviet government contended in every way. The United States, the giant capitalist nation which had emerged supreme from the war, with atomic weapons, was feared not only physically but also for her cultural, political, and economic ideas.

The main charge against artists now was that they had retrogressed to experiments in formalism and modernism and were not adhering to the tenets of socialist realism.

"The aim of literature," Zhdanov insisted, "is to help the state to educate the youth . . . and its purpose is to portray the Soviet man and his qualities in full force and completeness . . . in performing this task it must protect itself against the poisonous miasmas of Western bourgeois art. Soviet literature is the most advanced, progressive, and revolutionary literature of the world, and Soviet writers have to attack the degenerated, decadent bourgeois culture."[29]

Again the victims fell, individuals and whole institutions. Anna Akhmatova (1888–1966), a poet, and Mikhail Zoshchenko (1895–1958), a short-story writer, were censored and finally expelled from

29. Slonim, *Russian Theater*, p. 363.

the writers' union. Expulsion meant economic reprisal and social disgrace because only approval from the union could bring royalties and assignments from publishing houses. Akhmatova's poetry was condemned as too erotic, mystical, and apathetic. Zoshchenko was derided for his satires and for failing to contribute to the war effort in an appropriate way.

But this was only the beginning.

The theater world was shaken by the dismissal of Alexander Tairov, the head of the Moscow Chamber Theater. Like other Moscow theaters, his had failed to produce enough plays on contemporary Soviet themes. Tairov's theater was closed in 1949 and he died a year later.

At the same time that progressive directors were being banished from the stage, a new theory—the no-conflict theory—was emerging for drama. The new doctrine was a party argument that socialism had reached such a high state of development that there were no longer any internal enemies to be depicted on stage. Plays now were to deal only with the glorious achievements of society, without any conflicts whatever.

It was a deadly doctrine, and not even a consistent one. By 1952 even Soviet critics were deriding the dullness and boredom of the theater and asking, naturally, for a little more conflict. The problems of the playwright whose guidelines were redrawn every few years were crippling. He had to satisfy himself artistically, but his reputation and even survival required that he correctly anticipate the doctrines and policies his work would promote and oppose. If he guessed wrong, he was always at fault—rarely the critic or the party.

The motion picture directors Vsevolod Pudovkin and Sergei Eisenstein were attacked also. Eisenstein was held guilty for his interpretation of Ivan the Terrible as a "weak-willed Hamlet." He had produced very little in the 1930s after severe reprimands from the party. In the ten years before his death in 1948, he made only two movies, *Alexander Nevsky* (1938) and *Ivan the Terrible* (1945–1946), trying deliberately to confine himself to historical topics. For *Alexander Nevsky* Stalin is reported to have slapped Eisenstein on the back and remarked, "Sergei Mikhailovitch, you're a good Bolshevik after all." *Ivan the Terrible* must have shown him that there was no safety even in history. He died two years later.

A scene from Eisenstein's movie *Ivan the Terrible*. *Sovfoto*

The party campaign against films led to the scrapping of 85 percent of the movies produced in 1947. Everything had to be reap-
praised and most work was condemned to the trash can. In 1948 no
more than fifteen films were released; in 1949, only six; in 1950,
eleven; in 1951, nine; and in 1952, nine. The basic problem for the
scenarist was to write a script with an acceptable ideology that
would also provide entertainment. In the desperate search for the

Sergei Prokofiev,
a drawing by Henri Matisse.
The Bettmann Archive

right path, it was not unusual for scenarists to send their scripts straight to Stalin's Kremlin headquarters for approval.

The attack on composers came eighteen months later, but it was not less virulent. When the ax fell, it struck not only a little-known Georgian composer, Vano Muradeli, but also the world-famous Sergei Prokofiev, Dmitri Shostakovich, and Aram Khatchaturian. The party was not only critical but abusive. It described Muradeli's opera, *The Great Friendship*, as "vicious and inartistic in both its music and its subject matter." The opera's description of the peoples of the Caucasus was proclaimed "historically false and fictitious." The great crime of Muradeli, Shostakovich, Prokofiev, and Khatchaturian was that they were "formalists," dabbling around with "discordant noises wholly strange to the normal human ear and oppressive to the listener."[30]

The composers were accused of forgetting "how to write for the people" and of not producing a contemporary Russian opera comparable to the Russian classics. In one sense this was merely the application of the doctrine of socialist realism to music. Although no music is ever "realistic," the party chiefs obviously wanted recognizable tunes, easily sung melodies, and program music that would glorify Russian and Soviet achievements.

30. George S. Counts and Nucia Lodge, *The Country of the Blind: The Soviet System of Mind Control* (Boston: Houghton Mifflin, 1949), as quoted in Andrei Olkhovsky, *Music Under the Soviets* (New York: Praeger, 1955), pp. 280, 281.

But, in another sense, in music as in the other arts, the party officials were only echoing the world-wide popular cry that usually
greets new styles of artistic expression. The difference in Russia
has been that the conventional tastes of popular culture have been
elevated to the level of official doctrine and then propagated and
enforced with the power of government. Whereas in other societies
an innovative artist must overcome the resistance of critics, patrons,
and audiences, in the Soviet Union today he is hardly ever given
the chance to try his wings in public unless he somehow assuages
the traditional tastes of officialdom. On and off through the years the
greatest Soviet composers, men such as Shostakovich and Prokofiev,
have tried to balance these conflicting pressures, producing music
that was simultaneously daring in its rhythms and harmonies yet
respectful of Russian folk songs and political themes.

Unlike music, the graphic arts evoked no special resolution from
the party's central committee, but the line—and the effect—in the
art world was the same as in the other creative professions. The
party wanted complete control over the painters and sculptors.

Ehrenburg, in his memoirs, describes the party's attitude toward
Robert Falk, a modernist painter of the 1920s who had emigrated
to Paris but then returned to the Soviet Union in 1935. Falk's style
was basically realist but he used color to create shapes and space in
unusual ways. "In 1946 or 1947," Ehrenburg writes, "Falk was classed
as a 'formalist.' This was absurd, but in those days nothing much
surprised one. He was to be brought to his knees. I remember one of
the leaders of the artists' union in those days saying: 'Falk doesn't
understand words, we shall hit his pocket.' This really amazed me
even at that time: the man did not realize with whom he was dealing. I have never in my life met a painter so indifferent to all material things—to comfort, to money. Falk cooked himself peas or po-
tatoes; he went about for years in the same shabby coat; he wore one
shirt, and his only other lay in an old suitcase. . . . His pictures were
no longer shown. He was penniless. He might have been buried
alive. But he went on working. Sometimes art lovers or young painters would visit his studio: he welcomed them all, talked about art,
and smiled deprecatingly."[31]

31. Ehrenburg, *op. cit.*, p. 315.

Anti-semitism, always an undercurrent in Soviet politics, was a discernible characteristic of the purges. After an article in *Pravda,* the party newspaper, in January 1948, attacking the "antipatriotic group of dramatic critics," several Jewish critics in Moscow were arrested. Jewish language theaters were closed, and the popular actor Mikhoels and other Jewish intellectuals were arrested. Mikhoels died in 1948 and was later accused of "cosmopolitanism" and espionage for "Zionism." Jews figured prominently in artistic circles and they were particularly vulnerable to the charge of "cosmopolitanism," since they all knew other Jews scattered in all parts of the world.

The Jews' position in Russia was an anomaly even in czarist times and certainly under Stalin. Under the czars Jews could only live within the Pale, a section along the western border of Russia. With few exceptions they could not live in the capital cities of Moscow and St. Petersburg, and pogroms, or massacres, were regularly conducted against them. Possibly because of these repressions, Jews were active in the various socialist and revolutionary movements and some, like Leon Trotsky, were prominent in the Revolution of 1917.

Although the Soviets condemned all religions and at first prohibited religious observance, Jews were always forced to maintain a separate identity as one of the two hundred ethnic groups in the Soviet Union. They had to list themselves as Jews on internal passports that all Soviet citizens carry no matter how they thought of themselves or where they lived. In the 1930s they were "given" a small territory, Birobidzhan, in eastern Siberia, to call their own, but the Jews, who had lived for centuries in western Russia, never moved in large numbers to this artificial creation.

Stalin had a special resentment for Jews. In 1952 he had the Jewish writers David Bergelson, Lieb M. Kvitko, and Perets D. Markish executed. In 1952–1953 he uncovered a "doctors' plot," for which he blamed the mysterious death of Andrei Zhdanov in 1948. Most of the imprisoned doctors were Jews and they were found innocent after Stalin's death.

There was no public acknowledgment of anti-semitism in the Soviet Union, but Nikita Khrushchev, Stalin's successor, is known to have said in 1962 it was better for Jews not to hold high posts in government, for this only stirs popular resentment. Khrushchev added that in his opinion the unrest in Poland and Hungary in 1956 had been caused by the large number of Jews in high places.[32]

Khrushchev's remarks grew out of his reprimand to Dmitri Shostakovich, a non-Jew, for having chosen as the theme for his Thirteenth Symphony five poems by the popular poet Yevgeni Yevtushenko, including *Babi Yar*. This poem is about a ravine in Kiev, where thirty-four thousand Jews were slaughtered by the Germans in September 1941. It asks why the Russians, who had erected all kinds of war monuments, had not erected one in honor of the Jews slain at Babi Yar. The poem implied that anti-semitism still existed in the Soviet Union and that the lack of a memorial was a deliberate policy of the Soviet authorities.

Under extreme pressure to soften this charge and to make possible the performance of the symphonic cantata, Yevtushenko agreed to make textual changes and Shostakovich adjusted the score.

Babi Yar was omitted from the 1970 edition of Yevtushenko's collected poems and the altered symphony, which was initially performed in 1962, has been rarely heard in Russia since.

The purges of the forties ended with Stalin's death, but not until thousands of people had been jailed, sent to labor camps, or executed, among them hundreds of artists. More than six hundred writers were later "rehabilitated," but only half of these survived imprisonment to return home.

Since 1953: One Step Forward, Two Steps Back

Soviet cultural life since 1953 has been like a game of Giant Steps: one step forward, toward freedom, two steps back. After Stalin's death the artists dared to hope that the tenets of socialist realism, the purges, and the ideological conformity that he had imposed would also die.

The artists have been alternately confirmed and disappointed in this hope. With or without Stalin there appears to be a limit to the freedom that the leaders of the Communist party will allow. Even though the Soviet people have grown vastly more sophisticated and

32. *Problems of Communism*, Supplement, July/August 1963, p.v.

educated since socialist realism was first proclaimed, the party leadership continues to value it as a prescription for ideological conformity and political orthodoxy.

The party's basic fear is that cultural diversity will ignite demands for political diversity as well. Refusing to recognize any challenge to its political authority, the Communist party is afraid to surrender authority in any field.

Still, the obvious need to dissolve the atmosphere of repression that Stalin bequeathed produced some better days for artists. When Khrushchev finally prevailed over his rivals and took charge of the party, he permitted a relaxation of controls so as to stimulate the economy and win support for his effort to "overtake" the capitalist West.

Thus the middle years of the 1950s came to be known as "the thaw," from a novel of that title by the journalist-novelist Ilya Ehrenburg (1891–1967), published in 1954. *The Thaw* was remarkable not only for what it said, but for who was saying it. Ehrenburg, a member of the Communist party, had been, since his return to Russia in 1924, a zealous follower of the party line. This had made some of his literary colleagues suspicious, but it conferred added meaning on *The Thaw*. Ehrenburg broke with the tradition of depersonalized industrial and agricultural fiction, and depicted instead the life and loves of a small town. Ordinary people were shown expressing doubts, hopes, and desires; characters were not black and white caricatures of bad and good people, but complex composites of gray.

It seemed that with Stalin's death, Ehrenburg shook off a shadow which had constrained his literary endeavors. At the writers' congress in December 1954, he said: "You read novels where everything is in its place, every detail of the machine and of production meetings is properly described . . . but where's the human soul? . . . I do not delude myself! I know that in *The Thaw* as in my other books there is much that is imperfect, indeed unfinished. But what I reproach myself with is very different from the reproaches which have been made to me by the critics. If I am still able to write another book I will try to see to it that it is a step forward and not a step aside from my last novel. . . ."[33]

---

33. From book jacket of Soviet edition of *The Thaw*.

In his next books, his memoirs entitled *Men, Years—Life*, Ehrenburg described with increasing candor the events of the tumultuous century. And with equal courage he championed in the last decades of his life the rebirth of creative freedom.

The congress at which Ehrenburg spoke was the first one held since the formation of the Union of Soviet Writers in 1934, even though the bylaws of the organization called for triennial meetings. In the twenty years between congresses, membership in the union had grown from 1,500 to 3,695, reflecting in part the increased number of representatives from various non-Russian nationalities in the Soviet Union. Party spokesmen reaffirmed socialist realism as the guiding principle of literature but dissenting voices were raised in criticism of the "no-conflict theory" in the theater and the "gray flood of colorless, mediocre literature which has swept in the last few years over our literary magazines and is inundating the book market."[34]

Although the writers' congress did not mark a sharp break with doctrine, a simultaneous meeting of architects did just that. Soviet architecture, like the other arts, had been forced to renounce the modernism of the 1920s and to turn back in time to find appropriate styles for the new state. The appropriate style of building came to be a neoclassicism relying heavily on stone pillars, cornices, and friezes. The standard plan of a mammoth tower, topped by a red Soviet star and flanked by two low-lying wings, was duplicated seven times in Moscow alone and replicas of it were built in other Soviet cities as well as in Warsaw, the capital of newly Communist Poland. The interest in pompous embellishment extended also to the Moscow subway, opened in 1935. Stained glass windows, paintings, and sculptures decorate the clean halls of this efficient rail system designed to serve also, by its depth, as an air raid shelter.

But by 1954, massiveness was an outdated style, if not aesthetically, then certainly economically. Stalin's habit of clearing city blocks for new skyscraper office buildings, and the destruction caused by World War II had created a great housing shortage in Russia's major cities. The new leader's attention turned toward satisfying consumer demands, and to satisfying them quickly and inexpensively.

34. *Problems of Communism*, March/April 1955, p. 9.

A Moscow subway station. The artistic panels portray major events in the history of the Ukrainian people. *Tass from Sovfoto*

Khrushchev accused the former head of the Academy of Architects of having "stifled the voices raised against embellishments and sham details in architecture." He cited as an example the two million rubles spent to build a spire in front of the city hall in Sverdlovsk. Angered, Khrushchev noted that "two schools for four hundred pupils each could have been built with the funds expended on the spire alone. . . . Where is the economic logic?"[35]

A year later, dismayed at the slow pace by which this criticism had been absorbed by the architects, the party's central committee decreed the demotion or dismissal of several of Russia's most famous architects—the designers of the Volga Don Canal, the Moscow subway stations, Moscow's tallest skyscrapers. Architecture, too, turned out to be a risky career and there was no way of "rewriting" one's work. In its haste now, the party that had frowned on foreign influences ordered its builders to study Western architecture.

35. *Ibid.*, July/August 1956, p. 30.

The Volga Don Canal.
Sovfoto

The reflexes of the architectural community were swift. The granite facade on a Kiev skyscraper was scrapped. Hundreds of buildings in the planning and building stage were shorn of their ornamentation.

To meet their vast housing needs, Russian architects now pioneered in the development of precast concrete. But when it came to construction of the modern, glass-walled Hall of Congresses, within the Kremlin walls, the Russian government sought the help of Italian architects, just as its czarist forebears had.

In justifying his architectural reforms, Khrushchev condemned Stalin in 1956 for his "cult of personality," for the purges, and for his reigns of terror. Now it was Stalin's turn to be purged. His name disappeared from streets and cities. His body was removed from the mausoleum on Red Square, which he had shared with Lenin. His statues and pictures were taken down from town squares and hotel lobbies.

"De-Stalinization," which had been in effect since 1953 in spite of minor policy fluctuations, was now official.

The effects of de-Stalinization were observed most clearly in literature and films, and less in music and painting. In all branches of art, however, there were "rehabilitations" of those who had been purged or exiled by Stalin.

Without explanation of what had happened to them or when, the government announced that it was now all right to publish and read writers such as Babel, Bolgakov, and Bergelson, the theater director Meyerhold, and a host of others. Prokofiev and Shostakovich were "cleared" of the attacks made in 1948, as was the poet Anna Akhmatova. The emigré author Bunin, a favorite among the older generation of Soviet authors such as Paustovsky and Fedin, was published again. The writer Olesha returned from exile in Central Asia. Even Western authors such as Hemingway were reintroduced to the Soviet public.

Artistic works as well as people were rehabilitated. Mayakovsky's satiric plays *The Bathhouse* and *The Bedbug* were staged again. Dmitri Shostakovich's second opera, *Katerina Izmailova*, was revised and revived.

The clearing of his name alleviated some of the pressures Shostakovich must have felt. He is one of those Soviet artists who creates in silence, "for the drawer," when blocked in public. Yet to make his peace with the party he had allowed himself to be used, without conviction, much as famous persons endorse commercial products in the United States.

One of Shostakovich's colleagues, Dmitri Kabalevsky (1905–), has had less trouble adjusting to party policies, partly because he rarely attempted to compose universal works in daring new idioms and rhythms. With Tikhon Khrennikov, former first secretary of the composers' union, and Aram Khatchaturian, an Armenian composer, he has dominated the post-war music scene. A teacher, critic, pianist, conductor, composer, and secretary of the union, Kabalevsky

Dmitri Kabalevsky. *Sovfoto*

is the winner of three Stalin prizes. He is well known for his piano compositions for children, which are often humorous.

De-Stalinization opened the floodgates on a whole range of previously unacceptable themes for literature.

In the forefront of the new writing was Vladimir Dudintsev's, *Not by Bread Alone,* a reaffirmation of the biblical idea that man exists not just by material things but by being true to himself and his faith. Dudintsev (1918–) uses a factory-industrial setting for his novel but, like Ehrenburg, he leaped far beyond the stereotypes of socialist realism. His work was truly realistic and critical.

The novel describes engineer Lopatkin's difficulties in winning approval for the design of a pipe-casting machine. The chief obstacle in his battle is the head of his factory, Drozdov, who refuses to fight with his superiors in Moscow even though he knows the new machine is a great advance. In the end, Lopatkin wins not only the bureaucratic fight but also his boss's wife.

Dudintsev's plot was sharply condemned by Khrushchev, who felt the author had shown only the negative side of Soviet life. But Khrushchev must have sympathized privately with the critique of Soviet bureaucrats. For he himself was always torn between frustration with party functionaries and dependence on them for the preservation of party control.

Publicly disagreeing with Khrushchev's attack on the novel was Konstantin Paustovsky (1892–1968), a pre-revolutionary writer known for his lyrical, apolitical stories. He and Ehrenburg often came to the support of the new literature, out of conviction and because their age and fame guaranteed them a certain immunity from persecution.

Paustovsky sided with Dudintsev because he thought there had arisen "a new caste of petit bourgeois . . . a new group of acquisitive carnivores, a group which has nothing in common either with the revolution, or with our regime, or with socialism. . . ." Trying to claim the right to criticize even high government officials, he further defined the new villains as uncultured, servile, interested only in profiteering, and without regard for the natural resources of the country. He described a trip he took on the steamship *Pobeda:* "Half of the passengers (intellectuals, painters, writers, workers, people connected with the theater) made up one social stratum, occupying the second- and third-class accommodations. The deluxe and first-class cabins were occupied by another social stratum: deputy ministers, very high-placed administrative officials, and other very exalted passengers. We did not and we could not have any contact with these passengers" who were "unbearable by their dismal arrogance, their total indifference to everything except their own position and their personal vanity."[36]

In spelling out so clearly who the Drozdovs were, Paustovsky explained why Dudintsev's book was as popular with the people as it was unpopular with the party.

Besides Dudintsev, Victor Nekrasov and Yuri Bondarev also wrote in the critical realist style, exploring the injustices of Soviet society. Other writers dealt with the personal relations among people and especially with the "right to love, even in situations that break up families, and the denial of the party's right to interfere with such attachments."[37]

Russian theatergoers were delighted with the chance to see Pogodin's *Sonnet of Petrarch* for, in dealing with a love affair between a married middle-aged engineer and a young laboratory technician, it scored a small triumph over the puritanical restraints of party dogma. Victor Rozov and Alexander Arbuzov also produced dramas dealing with everyday life. Their plays, almost devoid of politics, featured romance and marital relations.

From plays dealing with ordinary life, the process of literary evolution led to poetry and prose emphasizing the individual.

Yevgeni Yevtushenko and Andrei Voznesensky have been leaders of this new tendency. With Vasily Aksyonov, Bulat Okhudzhava, and Robert Rozhdestvensky they comprise the nearest thing in recent decades to an avant-garde of Soviet literature. They continued the tradition of Mayakovsky's futurists by adopting no fixed style but searching constantly for new word patterns and experimental phrasing. Boris Pasternak inspired several of them.

Yevtushenko (1933–) achieved great stature in the Soviet Union as well as in the West because of his clearly political themes. He has

36. Hugh McLean and Walter N. Vickery, trans. and eds., *The Year of Protest, 1956. An Anthology of Soviet Literary Materials* (New York: Vintage Books, 1961), pp. 156, 157.
37. *Problems of Communism,* September/October 1962, p. 40.

Yevgeni Yevtushenko reciting his poetry. *Tass from Sovfoto*

fought for creative freedom, has talked back to party leaders, and has been chastised by them. Generations to come will probably remember him less for his poetry than for his political activity on poetry's behalf. Yevtushenko well understands that if literature is politics in the Soviet Union, then the poet must be a politician if he is to survive with dignity.

In the 1960s he, Voznesensky, and Okhudzhava, a guitar-playing poet, revived Mayakovsky's custom of reciting poetry in public. Sometimes in Moscow's Mayakovsky Square, sometimes in packed soccer stadiums, they declaim their poetry to enthusiastic audiences who come not just to hear the lines and see the famous young idols, but also to receive a social, almost political, message. Deprived of a free press, under czarism as well as communism, Russians have long obtained some of their political awareness from literature instead of their newspapers.

Of a more philosophical bent than the others, Voznesensky mocks the strange curves that life takes in this excerpt from his "Parabolical Ballad":

> Fortunes like rockets fly routes parabolical,
> Rainbows less widespread than gloom diabolical.
>
> For instance, the fiery-red painter Gauguin,
> Bohemian, though sales-agent until then:
> To get to the Louvre from nearby Montmartre
> He looped through Tahiti, just missing Sumatra.
>
> Sped skyward, forgetting of money-born madness,
> Of cackling wives and of stifling academies.
> And so
>   he surmounted
>   terrestrial gravity.
> The priests of the fine arts were eager to have
>   at him:
> "A parabola's fine, but a straight line's far
>   shorter.
> Better copy old Eden," they scoffed over porter.
> But Gauguin zoomed away like today's rocketeers
> In a wind that went tearing at coat-tails and ears
> And entered the Louvre not through the front door,
>
> But crashed his parabola through ceiling and floor!
>
> Each reaches his truth with his own share
>   of nerve:
> A worm through a chink
>   and a man by a curve . . .[38]

38. Vladimir Ognev and Dorian Rottenberg, comps., *Fifty Soviet Poets* (Moscow: Progress Publishers, 1969), p. 131.

Andrei Voznesensky.
Tass from Sovfoto

The political concerns of his colleague, Rozhdestvensky, are revealed in *Radiation Sickness:*

Radiation sickness!
                 Humanity
puts it bluntly:
                     learn to endure.
The treatment
Takes an eternity,
and there's little chance
of a cure.
Judgment's passed.
No hope,
not a glimmer.
Is it fair—
               come, speak up and say—
that the heirs
of the Hiroshimas
for their fathers
               are made to pay? . . .

Drops of dew
have a poisonous glitter,
and the air
pretends to be clean.
The complaints
          of the guiltless
                          are bitter,
malformed infants
moan and scream.
Mauled by time,
               our ancient planet
is a gaping wound.
                    You are
omnipresent,
               and many-handed,
radiation sickness;
               your scars
never heal.
Look!
          The calendar, grinning crookedly,
sheds its sheets . . .
                    The deadly blast
fades away with the years,
                    but, wickedly,
time itself
you seek
to outlast.
In our blood-stream you rove,
                    sowing panic,
to our marrow
          you eat
               your way,
like the germ
of an epidemic,
like the curse
of a blighted day.
You attack us in secret.
               Your villainy,

like your sores,
is not pretty to see,
radiation sickness
                    of calumny
swagger,
cowardice, spiteful glee!
It's a fact,
                not a fruit of fantasy,
I am not
        sending words,
                        down the drain.
Look how beardless
                these days
                        is hypocrisy:
it's a sign
you've cropped up again:
Radiation sickness—
                how lavishly
You bestow your bounty.
                        Alas:
Exhortations won't help to banish you
from the planet's
tormented face.
There's no drug
in the medical cabinet,
there's no doctor
                to spell your doom.
Time will kill you
                in time.
That's definite.
It's a pity
it won't be soon.[39]

Lyricists are yet another group that distinguish the recent Soviet
literary scene. Until his death, Konstantin Paustovsky was patron of
the novelist Yuri Kazakov, the short-story writer Yuri Nagibin, and
the poet Bella Akhmadulina (who had been married to Yevtushenko
and is now married to Nagibin). In style the lyricists pattern them-

39. *Ibid.*, pp. 377, 379, 381.

selves after the terse, succinct prose of Ivan Bunin and Anton Chekhov. Their stories and pleas concentrate not on politics but on emotions: sadness at death, confusion upon growing up, loneliness. Theirs is almost a timeless rendering of the world of love and hate, joy and grief, divorced from everyday conditions, society, or history.

In her poem, "December," Bella Akhmadulina describes the joy of making a snowman:

> The rules of winter we obey.
> We roll a snowball and run after,
> Acclaim its growth with peals of laughter,
> And brush the surplus snow away.
>
> As if misfortune were in view,
> The people passing by assemble
> Along the fence with lips atremble
> To watch what you and I shall do.
>
> We make a snowman—that is all!
> O what a triumph when from under
> Your hands appears the chosen wonder,
> To your prescription, stout and tall!
>
> You say: "Just look what I can do!"
> I notice with what skill and passion
> From formlessness new form you fashion
> And say: "I love you, I love you!"
>
> With what exactness snow can trace
> The very features we intended!
> Then suddenly I see resplendent,
> The sidelong profile of your face.
>
> Scorning the crowd we walk away
> Across the year with self-possession.
> With such a child's intent expression
> May you, beloved, always play!
>
> To his long-lasting labour yield,
> O handiwork of my beloved!
> Grant the reward a child discovers
> On painting flowers in a field![40]

40. *Ibid.,* pp. 53, 55.

Communist critics define lyricism as "objective" art, not in the sense of telling the truth but for its mood of noninvolvement. Alongside the deeply committed, agitational quality of socialist realism, objectivism is neuter, art without political relevance, art for art's sake.

The avant-garde and the lyricists represent the most progressive element in Soviet letters today. Together with colleagues in other disciplines—Ernst Neizvestny, an abstract sculptor, Andrei Volkonsky, a composer who works in the twelve-tone scale, and Yuri Lyubimov, director of the Taganka Theater—they form an alliance aimed at linking Soviet and Western culture. Though they criticize their society, they are committed to the idea of socialism. They love their country, insisting that they show that love in their anguish over the society's moral and spiritual condition.

These "Westernizers" are opposed, as always in Russia, by the Slavophiles who deem Russia's own heritage a sufficient source of culture. Ilya Glazunov, a young painter, believes that "Picasso is not the new word in culture but the destruction of the old. From my point of view, jazz is the deeply national ritual music of primitive Negro tribes. I don't understand why primitive art and the effort to copy it must be considered the international art of the twentieth century."[41] He regards Russia's loss of individuality and assimilation of Western culture as the result of a great historical misstep.

Some of the Russian traditionalists, especially Alexander Solzhenitsyn and Vladimir Tendryakov, are thought to be the most talented in contemporary Soviet literature. "Like the Slavophiles . . . they are attracted by the symbols of 'eternal Russia,' chiefly the Orthodox church and the Russian village." Yet, "they are more mature, less chauvinistic with respect to non-Russian influences, and considerably more committed to the eradication of Stalinist blights,"[42] writes a British critic.

Thus the period of thaw, although interrupted by many more recent periods of repression and political pressure, has produced a broad spectrum of aesthetic and cultural viewpoints. Socialist realism, as the single all-inclusive standard of literature, has almost

41. *Problems of Communism,* March/April 1961, p. 43.
42. *Ibid.,* March/April 1967, p. 30.

disappeared, even though its tenets are still observed in the writings of Vsevolod Kochetov and Ivan Shevtsov among others. Poems praising Russia's past leaders still prevail, such as this one by Nikolai Tikhonov (1896–) about Lenin:

> Where firs by snow all silvered stand,
> Where palms grow in the golden south,
> From home to home, from land to land,
> His words pass on from mouth to mouth.
>
> On shores both near and far away,
> By more than one new generation
> In all five continents, today
> His name is held in veneration.
>
> He is enthroned in peoples' hearts,
> And is beloved in every clime.
> In one, though, he commenced his path
> Unheard of since the birth of time.
>
> A land where grief and fury reigned,
> Where peals of brewing thunder rolled,
> And where he loved his native tongue,
> Its mines of eloquence untold.
>
> He loved her skies, her steppes so vast,
> Her mounting wind of liberty . . .
> What can be nobler than to love
> One's native land as Lenin did.[43]

The variety of literature is accommodated in a large number of monthly magazines. These can usually be identified with a particular style or viewpoint, depending on their editors. *Novy Mir,* under the "liberal" editors Alexander Tvardovsky and Konstantin Simonov, has been a haven for progressive authors such as Dudintsev, Solzhenitsyn, and Nekrasov. *Oktyabr,* edited by Vsevolod Kochetov, has been clearly conservative. Theaters, too, have often evolved political or philosophical personalities. Yet the official outlets have not satisfied all writers, and a large underground literature has grown

43. *Fifty Soviet Poets,* p. 477.

Alexander Tvardovsky.
Tass from Sovfoto

up as well. Known as *samizdat* (self-published), this literature appears in various typewritten and mimeographed forms. The names of the underground journals—*Syntax, The Phoenix, Russian Word*—often signify the political aspect of their battle for literary freedom. *Russian Word* was first founded in 1859 and it spread the radical reform ideas of the 1860s. Although such publications are illegal and bring risk of punishment for editors, authors, and readers alike, they flourish in the Soviet Union today.

Even more than young rebels in the West, young Russians constantly debate the wisdom of operating "within the system," or trying to work against it underground. To press for more liberty, younger writers and artists have succeeded in electing some representatives to the boards of the artistic unions. Known as "revisionists" because they wish to revise doctrines governing Soviet art, they constantly challenge the authority of conservatives and party supporters and therefore operate in precarious circumstances.

If the thesis that literature is politics in the Soviet Union needed any proof, it was provided by Soviet reaction to the awarding of Nobel prizes to four of its famous authors: Ivan Bunin in 1933, Boris Pasternak in 1958, Mikhail Sholokhov in 1965, and Alexander Solzhenitsyn in 1970.

The Nobel prize has been awarded by Sweden in most years since 1901 in literature, peace, and the sciences. It is a prestigious prize, valued at about $80,000.

When Ivan Bunin (1870–1953) received it, little notice was taken of the event in his homeland since he was no longer a Soviet citizen but an emigré who had lived in Paris since 1921. Educated in czarist Russia, a successor to the classical style of Tolstoy and Chekhov, and one of Chekhov's close friends, Bunin departed his native land in great bitterness over the Bolshevik revolution. His novels, among them *The Village*, a description of peasant life, and stories, such as "The Gentleman from San Francisco," about the relationship of life and death, are read today in the Soviet Union as the last surviving links between Russia's pre-revolutionary heritage and contemporary literature. Though Bunin was vilified during Stalin's life, he was re-habilitated after 1953 and has since been republished. As a precise, dispassionate recorder of life without regard to its social implications, Bunin is much admired by the younger generation of Soviet writers.

Bunin was an unusual emigré, because he continued to produce in exile. Often emigré authors, in adapting to a new society and con-quering a new language, become men without a country, unable to create in a strange environment. Bunin avoided this pitfall, per-haps because of his youthful traveling and writing in the Near and Far East.

The second Soviet Nobel prize winner, more typically, could not even contemplate life outside his homeland. Like the hero of his book, *Dr. Zhivago*, Pasternak (1890–1960) equated exile with death and absorbed all manner of abuse rather than leave his native soil. When, soon after the award was announced, the head of the Young Communist League encouraged Pasternak to become a "real emi-grant" and "go to his capitalist paradise," and when the Moscow section of the writers' union asked the government to strip "the traitor Pasternak" of his citizenship and expel him from the country, Pasternak responded with this letter to Premier Khrushchev: "I am tied to Russia by birth, by life, and by work. I cannot imagine my fate separated from and outside of Russia. Leaving my motherland would equal death for me, and that is why I ask that you do not take this final measure in relation to me. With my hand on my heart, I can say I have done something for Soviet literature and can be use-ful to it in the future."[44]

44. *New York Times*, November 2, 1958.

An early photograph
of Boris Pasternak.
Tass from Sovfoto

Although he was encouraged by the government to accept the prize
and to leave Russia, Pasternak did neither. He died two years later,
but his memory was to stay alive to plague the government that dis-
graced him.

The acclaim for Pasternak's book in the West probably upset the
Communist party even more than the book itself. First accepted for
publication in *Novy Mir,* but finally rejected for its hostility toward
the spirit of the 1917 revolution, the book was smuggled out of the
country by Pasternak and an Italian Communist publisher. This itself
was deemed criminal by the government, but what really rankled
was the Nobel committee's celebration of what the Soviet leaders
regarded as anti-Communist propaganda.

Dr. Zhivago is the story of the generation that grew up with the
1905 revolution and matured in the revolutions of 1917. It is the
tale of men and women of the intelligentsia who sympathize with
the ideals of the revolution, and even participate to some extent, but
become disenchanted with its violent methods and objectives. Some
escape from the turmoil and moral conflict to Europe or the Orient,

but Yuri Zhivago, a physician, is unable to flee the Russia he loves so well.

A panorama of the revolution and civil war from the point of view of the displaced intellectual community, *Dr. Zhivago* is also an autobiographical novel. Zhivago's family, like Pasternak's artist-father, Leonid, emigrates to Western Europe. Yuri, the book's hero, like Boris, the author, is incapable of making the wrench from home. Lara, the heroine of the novel, represents a real-life Lara, who helped Pasternak in his dealings with the Italian publisher. After Pasternak's death she and her daughter were imprisoned for a time on false charges of currency smuggling.

The Soviet authorities' reluctance to publish *Dr. Zhivago* was understandable. This personal novel, delving into the complex emotions of its revolutionary and bourgeois characters, lyrically written and by implication deeply critical of the revolution, was not for Soviet consumption.

In a letter rejecting the manuscript in 1956, the editorial board of the magazine *Novy Mir* wrote to Pasternak: "The spirit of your novel is that of nonacceptance of the socialist revolution. The general tenor of your novel is that the October Revolution, the civil war, and the social transformations involved did not give the people anything but suffering, and destroyed the Russian intelligentsia, either physically or morally." After praising the spirit of Pasternak's earlier poetry, the editors remarked upon the novel's literary qualities: "There are quite a few first-rate pages, especially where you describe Russian natural scenery with remarkable truth and poetic power. There are many clearly inferior pages, lifeless and didactically dry. They are especially rife in the second half of the novel. Yet we would rather not dwell on this aspect since, as we have mentioned at the beginning of the letter, the essence of our argument with you has nothing to do with aesthetic wrongdoings."[45]

But the novel's rejection in the Soviet Union only enhanced its success in the West.

On being informed in October 1958 that he had won the Nobel prize, Pasternak probably aggravated his problems by remarking:

45. Robert Conquest, *The Pasternak Affair: Courage of Genius* (Philadelphia: J.B. Lippincott, 1962), pp. 141–42, 162.

"To receive this prize fills me with great joy and also gives me great moral support. But my joy today is a lonely joy."[46] Even so he could not have anticipated the quality of the denunciations that were to descend on him and, the thaw notwithstanding, the campaign that the party waged against him.

The head of the Young Communist League denounced Pasternak as a "pig" who did what "even pigs do not do"—dirtied the place in which he eats and lives. All the creative unions were called to meetings to denounce Pasternak and to petition unanimously for his expulsion from the country. In addition, he was expelled from the writers' union.

Of the many denunciations, there was perhaps one that struck home, that of "internal emigré." This was a stock party phrase applied to those who lived and worked in the Soviet Union but who did not in any way support the aims of the society. It was aptly applied to Pasternak, whose gentleness of soul and loftiness of lyric made him an opponent of the tactics and aims of the Communist party. Descended from an upper middle-class artistic family, he became, in the 1920s, with Mayakovsky, a member of the group of poets known as the futurists. Their aim was to free poetry from symbolism and mysticism and revivify it with colloquial speech. In that tradition Pasternak's poetry is enriched by commonplace images and yet is very personal. In *Eve* he expresses his awe of woman:

> On shore the trees stand looking on
> While midday casts the clouds on bet
> Into the meditative pond
> For want of any other net.
>
> And like a net the sky sinks in
> The pensively expectant waters
> And into it the bathers swim,
> Fathers, mothers, sons and daughters.
>
> Then half a dozen girls come out
> Without a stir among the shoots
> And rivulets of water spout
> As they wring out their bathing suits.

46. *New York Times*, October 26, 1958.

And, firing the imagination,
The coils of fabric coil and twist
As though the serpent of temptation
Had really marked them for its nest.

O woman, on your looks I dote,
But have no mental blanks to fill;
You're like the stricture in a throat
Seized by an unexpected thrill.

You seem created as a draft,
A stanza from another sequence,
As if indeed the handicraft
Of somebody who knew no equals,

Made of my rib while asleep I lay,
You broke the clasping arms apart,
The very image of dismay,
A spasm that grips and wrings man's heart.[47]

When socialist realism was proclaimed, Pasternak sensed that his poetry would not fit the desired propagandistic format, and he took to translating Shakespeare's plays and the poetry of Stalin's Georgia.

Dr. Zhivago was conceived soon after World War II in the hope that life and artistic conditions would improve in the post-war period. But Pasternak was disappointed in more ways than one. Not only did Zhdanov resume the purges, but even Stalin's death did not end the vindictive treatment of writers.

But for his pains and troubles over *Dr. Zhivago,* Pasternak earned even more the respect of the younger poets, such as Yevgeni Yevtushenko and Andrei Voznesensky, and the literary critic, Andrei Sinyavsky. He became a martyr and a symbol of faith in literary integrity, as well as a poet to be emulated.

In the year of the Pasternak affair, three Soviet scientists traveled to Stockholm with great fanfare to receive their Nobel awards. The Soviet attack on the Nobel Academy focused only on its literary selections. And even in this respect the objections were particular, rather than general. In 1965 Mikhail Sholokhov was allowed to ac-

47. *Fifty Soviet Poets,* pp. 351, 353.

Nobel Prize Laureate
Mikhail Sholokhov.
Sovfoto

cept the once-scorned literary prize for his novels *And Quiet Flows
the Don* and *Virgin Soil Upturned.*

Sholokhov (1905–), despite his reputation as the Soviet Union's
most popular author, despite the sales of his books into the millions,
and despite the fact that Nikita Khrushchev took him as his personal
guest on a tour of the United States in 1959, has also known troubles
with the party's literary standards.

Unlike Bunin and Pasternak, Sholokhov is of mixed peasant and
Cossack origin and at an early age became a Communist. His famous novels, dealing with the civil war and the collectivization of
the farms, meet "socialist-realist" requirements both in content and
style.

But problems arose over the party's demand that socialist realist
heroes be positive and optimistic to the end, while villains be drawn
negatively, without any redeeming features. For Communist party
critics the fact that the powerful and sympathetic hero of *And Quiet
Flows the Don,* Grigory Melekhov, has still not become a Bolshevik
at the end of the book posed a serious crisis of standards. How could

even this good book be acceptable if the hero refuses to come over to the Communist party? How had it been possible, in the early volumes of the book, to become so emotionally involved with this "enemy"? The critics finally solved their dilemma by declaring *And Quiet Flows the Don* a tragedy, making it unnecessary, they argued, for the victorious Bolsheviks to empathize with the vanquished, recalcitrant peasants.

The ending of *Virgin Soil Upturned* also caused trouble for Sholokhov, who tried to make his books dramatically true and genuine. The first volume of this novel about collectivization in the Don region appeared in 1932, but the second part was returned for "revisions" in 1936. Almost twenty years later, in 1955, the initial chapters of the second part finally appeared but it was not until 1960 that the ending could be published.

Prior to publication, rumors circulated in Moscow that Sholokhov had originally intended the hero, Davydov, to be killed in the purges of the 1930s. When the book finally appeared, however, Davydov was killed in an attempt to capture some anti-Soviet plotters.

Sholokhov further obliged the party by "revising" *And Quiet Flows The Don* for its 1955 edition to appease the party's increasingly virulent anti-Western policy.

Not only did the party profit from these textual revisions but Sholokhov did, too, for in calculating book royalties, each revision counts as a new book.

In spite of his problems with the party over his plots, Sholokhov remains a staunch Communist. His recent speeches at writers' congresses are violently critical of colleagues, such as Solzhenitsyn, who have refused to compromise their art with party demands. Still, the long delays in his own literary activity suggest that he was similarly troubled by the conflicting aims of politics and literature. But he seems to have resolved his dilemma in a way satisfactory to the party and himself.

Twelve years after the Pasternak affair, the Soviet government was plagued by another Nobel prize that it could not accept or approve politically. The winner, the novelist Alexander Solzhenitsyn (1918–), strangely benefited from the virulent campaign that had been waged against Pasternak. Mindful of world public opinion and its adverse reaction to the treatment of Pasternak, the Soviet govern-

Alexander Solzhenitsyn throws dirt into grave of Alexander Tvardovsky during funeral. *United Press International Photo*

ment this time directed its protests not against the author of *The Cancer Ward* and *The First Circle* but against the committee that had awarded him the prize. It condemned the choice as politically motivated. In any case, there was little left for the government to do; it had already had Solzhenitsyn expelled from the writers' union and made him jobless and destitute.

Solzhenitsyn had been an inmate of Stalin's labor camps, to which he was sent after writing a letter that referred to the former dictator as "the whiskered one." A survivor of eight years of camp life, Solzhenitsyn was amnestied in the mid-1950s, after Stalin's death, but he was denied permission to live in the western part of Russia for the rest of his life. In 1962 his novel, *One Day in the Life of Ivan*

Denisovich, about life in a Siberian labor camp, was personally approved by Khrushchev for publication in the magazine *Novy Mir.* At the time it seemed expedient to use the book to further tarnish Stalin's reputation by publicizing the excesses of his era. Within a year, however, Khrushchev thought it an error to have exposed Soviet readers to this autobiography of horror. The publication of similar books was stopped. From that time on Solzhenitsyn was denied an outlet for his writing, except for several short stories, also printed by *Novy Mir.* In Ryazan, where he taught mathematics, he continued to write novels, plays, and stories. His next novel, *The Cancer Ward* —about a camp survivor's bout with disease—was rejected for publication by *Novy Mir* despite an impassioned plea from the author that the work be published in his own country. Otherwise, he argued, and not through his own doing, typewritten copies of the novel would find their way to the West and be published without the approval of the Soviet government. Solzhenitsyn knew that this would be the greatest transgression an author could commit.

But he remained condemned to silence, which he refused to accept. Perhaps because of the hardships he had endured in the camps, and perhaps because of a seemingly miraculous recovery from stomach cancer, Solzhenitsyn appeared fearless. He petitioned the writers' congress for an end of censorship. He wrote another novel, *The First Circle,* about scientists who are kept as political prisoners. And he stood undaunted against government reprisals. In November 1969 he was ejected without a hearing from the local Ryazan writers' union and from the national union. Without even waiting for the "affront" of a Nobel award, the Soviets punished Solzhenitsyn in the same way they had punished Pasternak. Like Pasternak, he was told that he was free to leave the country. Like Pasternak, he saw his works printed abroad and gain wide popularity there.

By this time, however, there had developed a small but determined group of dissenters in the Soviet Union who objected to the control of the arts and to the unconstitutional methods of persecuting artists and scientists. Whereas Pasternak had been reviled during the last years of his life and had been shunned, even at death, by the literary elite, Solzhenitsyn found support for his literary integrity and also for his material needs. Since he could not be published, he had no income. But he was aided by the writer Kornei Chukhovsky—who, when he died, left him a legacy on which he subsisted for three years—and by the cellist Mstislav Rostropovich, among others. Rostropovich offered the novelist refuge in his summer *dacha,* or country house, and when criticism of the Nobel award appeared in the Soviet press, Rostropovich sent a letter to Soviet newspapers (which they did not print but which was later smuggled out to the West) pleading for every man's right to "think independently and express his opinion about what he knows, what he has personally thought about, experienced, and not merely to express with slightly different variations the opinion which has been inculcated in him."[48]

Solzhenitsyn accepted the Nobel award but decided not to travel to Stockholm to receive it. He cited the strain of the ceremonies and his own poor health. Above all, however, he was probably afraid that he would never be allowed to return to the Soviet Union. He still hopes—despite obstacles placed by his government—to obtain the Nobel prize money which would lighten his material concerns.

He also continues to write, now on historical, not personal, themes, with just as little possibility of being published in his own country. The first volume in his current series on World War I, *August 1914,* appeared abroad in 1971. It represents not only a literary, but a research, effort in the face of government refusal to make records, people, and buildings available to the author.

His love of his country undiminished by his hardships, Solzhenitsyn, like Pasternak, chooses to remain there at any cost.

In spite of the Pasternak affair in 1958, the Soviet cultural scene tipped back and forth in seesaw fashion, approaching but always retreating from real artistic freedom. The atmosphere seemed so positive in 1962 that the poet Bella Akhmadulina could say: "I think that the time has become happy for us, that it now runs in our favor. Not only can my comrades work, but they are given every encouragement in their endeavor."[49]

But, as before, the amnesty for writers was short-lived. The very next winter witnessed another decline in the writers' status. The con-

48. *New York Times,* November 16, 1970.
49. Priscilla Johnson, *Khrushchev and the Arts. The Politics of Soviet Culture, 1962–1964* (Cambridge, Mass.: MIT Press, 1965), p. 3.

servative careerists who had adhered to the party's "socialist realist" line pushed the younger liberals to the side again and aimed to take revenge.

Events were actually triggered at an art show of seventy-five canvases—modern and, by Soviet standards, even extreme canvases. Just as the young artists thought they had won a place at home at last, Khrushchev, the head of the party and the government, arrived with two conservative artists—Vladimir Serov and Sergei Gerasimov—and let fly an impassioned public critique of the work that further delayed the development of modern painting in the Soviet Union. "As long as I am president of the Council of Ministers," he said, "we are going to support a genuine art. We aren't going to give a kopeck for pictures painted by jackasses. History can be our judge. For the time being history has put us at the head of this state, and we have to answer for everything that goes on in it. . . . We are going to take these blotches with us into communism, are we? If government funds have been paid for this picture, the person who authorized it will have the sum deducted from his salary! Write out a certificate that this picture has not been acquired by the government. . . ."

And to the young creators of the paintings he said: "Just give me a list of those of you who want to go abroad, to the so-called 'free world.' We'll give you foreign passports tomorrow, and you can get out. Your prospects here are nil. What is hung here is simply anti-Soviet. It's amoral. Art should ennoble the individual and arouse him to action. . . . You're a nice-looking lad, but how could you paint something like this? We should take down your pants and set you down in a clump of nettles until you understand your mistakes. . . . We have the right to send you to cut trees until you've paid back the money the state has spent on you."[50]

Suddenly, a campaign was under way. Khrushchev followed with a policy address that was so sweeping in its discussion of the arts that it reminded many of the two-year campaign waged for Stalin by Andrei Zhdanov in 1946–1948. Socialist realism was upheld, the modern twelve-tone scale was decried as cacophonous; Yevtushenko, Ehrenburg, Nekrasov, were all attacked; the film industry was ac-

50. *Ibid.*, pp. 102–103.

cused of shortcomings; jazz was described as a "kind of music that gives you a feeling of nausea and pain in the stomach."[51]

Apparently sensitive to charges that he had been a collaborator of Stalin, Khrushchev countered by insisting that he had resisted the Stalin terror and by suggesting that Ehrenburg too had collaborated while his friends were being killed. And he condemned the makers of a movie, *The Gate of Ilyich,* because it stimulated a debate about guilt between Soviet fathers and sons. He went so far as to suggest that there had probably been too many memoirs written about Stalin's camps and purges.

Khrushchev denounced "objectivism" in art and generally defended the cultural policies of Stalin's day. Finally he gave the real signal: "At Stalin's funeral many, including myself, were in tears," he said. "These were sincere tears. Although we knew about some of Stalin's personal shortcomings, we believed in him."[52]

With this statement, de-Stalinization stopped.

Tighter restrictions on publishing followed the speech, as did "recantations" by some of the writers under attack. But the cold war between the conservatives who supported the party and the liberals continued. Each week, one group or the other scored a "victory" with the publication of a story or poem deemed reprehensible by the other. The trend, however, was conservative, and it accelerated after Khrushchev's fall from power in 1964.

Early in 1965, his successors—Leonid Brezhnev and Alexei Kosygin—set their course in cultural politics by putting on trial two writers who had pseudonymously sent work abroad for publication.

Attempts to deal with rebellious artists with verbal denunciations and economic sanctions had obviously failed. So the party reverted to police measures: the search of apartments, arrests, trials with prearranged verdicts of guilty, sentences to labor camps, and, in extreme cases, commitment of undesirable artists to insane asylums.

The trial of Abram Tertz and Nikolai Arzhak, alias Andrei Sinyavsky and Yuli Daniel, was to be the first of a series aimed at a whole group of dissidents in Moscow. The trial also sparked a small but formal movement of dissent that has spread from the artistic

51. *Ibid.,* p. 175.
52. *Ibid.,* p. 160.

Andrei Sinyavsky (*foreground*) and Yuli Daniel at their trial in 1966. *Tass from Sovfoto*

world to scientists and other scholars. The original dissenters sought only artistic freedom, but the methods used by the government to harass and punish them so stretched legal and judicial procedures that the movement broadened into a campaign for the reform of all Soviet society.

The first of the defendants, Andrei Sinyavsky, had led two distinct literary careers and achieved recognition in both. Publicly, he was a literary critic, highly respected in the Soviet Union. He was a graduate of Moscow University and his idol in his formative years was Boris Pasternak, that silent resister of the party's precepts.

Among Sinyavsky's credits as critic were the introduction to a collection of Pasternak's poetry, and articles on poetry for literary histories and encyclopedias.

He supported the younger generation of poets, Yevtushenko, Akhmadulina, Voznesensky, and stressed the need for individualism in art "to relate poetry to one's own experience . . . to find out one's own standpoint on reality."[53] He was a contributor to *Novy Mir* and, in addition to his literary interests, published a pamphlet popularizing the art of Picasso.

But, in another incarnation, for *samizdat* and Western consumption only, Sinyavsky was Abram Tertz, the creator of unusual tales about contemporary Soviet life. As he himself described his work in an essay *On Socialist Realism:* "Right now I put my hope in a phantasmagorical art, with hypothesis instead of a purpose, an art in which the grotesque will replace realistic description of ordinary life. Such an art would correspond best to the spirit of our time. May the fantastic imagery of Hoffmann and Dostoevsky, of Goya, Chagall, and Mayakovsky . . . teach us how to be truthful with the aid of the absurd and imaginary."[54]

Sinyavsky's codefendant was Yuri Daniel, publicly a translator of poetry from Slavic, Yiddish, and Caucasian languages. A satirist like Tertz, Daniel wrote for the underground under the name Nikolai Arzhak. A less important literary figure than Sinyavsky-Tertz, Daniel-Arzhak's crime in the eyes of Soviet authorities was his story, "This is Moscow Speaking," a day of decreed and legal murder in the Soviet Union.

While censorship, party control, and corrective labor camps have existed throughout the Communist years, Stalin's death ended the use of the death penalty against dissidents. The intellectual and artistic community learned this from Khrushchev's "lenient" treatment of Molotov, Kaganovich, and Malenkov, whom he overthrew in 1957. Instead of death, these political opponents were sentenced to exile or house arrest. Whether generous or merely defensive, the new policy benefited many others. Artists sensed that party disapproval would bring lesser punishments for them too. Emboldened by this knowledge, they continued to press the regime for creative freedom.

At their trial in February 1966, Sinyavsky and Daniel demonstrated this bold courage (or reckless sincerity). Their moral resist-

53. *Problems of Communism,* March/April 1966, p. 69.
54. Slonim, *Soviet Russian Literature,* p. 342.

ance, so different from the confessions during the purges of the 1930s, established a new precedent that other dissenters now follow.

The writers were accused of having sent their materials abroad. By itself this is not a crime in Soviet law. But according to Soviet authorities these works contained malicious slander of the Soviet Union, the export of which is a crime.

The trial resembled some of those of Stalin's day. After their arrest, the defendants had no legal counsel until the state's investigation and inquisition of them had been completed. Public attacks on the writers preceded the trial, although their arrest six months earlier had not received notice in the press. The trial audience was carefully selected, and even excluded representatives of the foreign Communist press. Official transcripts of the trial were doctored, and it was only from the shorthand notes taken down by some spectators that a record was smuggled to the West.

The philosophy of state control and the spirit of individual resistance that have prevailed side by side throughout Russian history can best be appreciated from these excerpts from the Sinyavsky–Daniel trial testimony:

Judge Smirnov: Do you understand the substance of the indictment?

Daniel: I do.

Judge: Do you plead guilty?

Daniel: No, neither in part nor in full.

Prosecutor Oleg Temushkin: Tell us, Defendant Daniel, what ideas were you trying to express in "Moscow Speaking"?

Daniel: I was interested in analyzing the psychology of people placed in an unusual situation. There were no political motives. It was pure psychology. You see, I wanted to draw a fantastic situation to put the characters into unusual conditions. It is, properly speaking, fantasy.

Prosecutor: Why did you not then choose another locale for the action, ancient Babylon for example? Why portray vile fantasies among your own people?

Daniel: This is an artistic method.

Judge: Who can seriously believe that the Soviet government would declare a "day of permissible murder"?

Daniel: If it is clear that no one could believe it, how could you suggest any slander is involved?

Judge: Slander is the deliberate circulation of false inventions. This means that what you wrote is slander.

Daniel: No, it is artistic hyperbole . . .

Prosecutor: Could your book be interpreted in an anti-Soviet sense? Could our enemies use it as a weapon in the struggle against our fatherland, our regime, our people?

Daniel: Yes, but a man must remain a man whatever the conditions, whatever the influences.

Prosecutor: Did this cause you any worry? Did you call back your latest work? Did you protest to the publishers?

Daniel: No, but I never consciously wanted to bring harm to my country. Only during the preliminary investigations did I understand that my works are directed against the regime and the epoch . . .

Some of the questions put to Sinyavsky were as follows:

Judge: Perhaps we can leave literary theory. We are not conducting a seminar on literary themes but criminal proceedings. You speak of the Soviet people as "creatures of blood and dirt." How can we reconcile that with your love for Communist ideals?

Sinyavsky: I think that is an incorrect translation.

Judge: Why did you send this monstrous slander out of the country?

Sinyavsky: I wanted to tell people about the nation's spiritual needs. I am not a political writer. I am far removed from politics.

Prosecutor: Let us return to your own thoughts, expressed not in fictional works but in literary, as you term them, meditations. You know the work *Thinking Aloud?*

Sinyavsky: That is my work.

Prosecutor: Was it published abroad?

Sinyavsky: Yes.

Prosecutor: Let me quote: "Drunkenness is the idée fixe of the Russian people . . ." "A nation of thieves and drunks incapable of creating a culture." What do you have to say about this?

Sinyavsky: You see, I love the Russian people. You could not accuse me of being partial to the West. I have even been called a Slavophile.

Prosecutor: Which works express your views, those published in this country or those published abroad?

Sinyavsky: I don't know exactly.

Prosecutor: In reply to the court's questions you have frequently said that you deny the anti-Soviet essence of your works. Why did you not try to publish these works in the Soviet Union?

Sinyavsky: My artistic tastes differ from those of the publishing houses. My works are complicated and intricate. It is difficult to see the logical essence of the images. I don't even know myself what they mean.[55]

Despite their protestations of love for their country and their insistence that authors must write as they see fit regardless of the consequences, Sinyavsky and Daniel were sentenced to seven and five years, respectively, in a labor camp.

It is not known how much camp conditions have changed since Stalin's day. In 1969 six writers—Yuri Daniel was one of them—who were serving prison terms in the Potma camp complex 250 miles east of Moscow, wrote a letter to the Supreme Soviet criticizing camp conditions and asking for reforms. They said they worked twelve to fourteen hours a day on a maximum diet of 2,413 calories, which they said was enough only for a sedentary person in normal conditions. They said the temperature in their living quarters was abnormally low, between thirty-two and fifty degrees Fahrenheit, except in summer. They also protested the inability of prisoners to marry or to write more than two letters a month. (In 1970, having served his term, Daniel was released from the camp.)

The Sinyavsky-Daniel trial set off a tragic chain of events. After the trials, a "white paper," or critical transcript, circulated in the underground press. Its author was Alexander Ginzburg, who sought to show that the trial verdict was predetermined. He roused many Soviet intellectuals to protest, at considerable risk to their own reputations and incomes.

In January 1967 the authorities arrested Ginzburg, Yuri Galanskov, the editor of *The Phoenix*, an underground magazine, and Vera Lashkova, the typist of their manuscripts.

In January-February 1967 three more young people were arrested

55. *New York Times*, February 15, 1966.

for having protested the arrests of Ginzburg, Galanskov, and Lashkova and having demanded the repeal of Article 70 of the criminal
code, which provides punishments for hostile "agitation or propaganda." One of them, Vladimir Bukovsky, a writer, had been arrested twice before for circulating underground literature, ending up
once in a prison-like mental home and the second time in a psychi-
atric ward near Moscow.

At his trial in September 1967, he delivered an eloquent defense,
insisting that he had broken no law and operated only in accordance
with the country's constitution. His final speech reached the West
through Pavel Litvinov, a grandson of Maxim Litvinov, a former
foreign minister and the first Soviet ambassador to the United States.
Litvinov had protested the trial of Ginzburg, Galanskov, and Lashkova, for which he lost his job as a chemist. One year later he himself
was tried and sentenced to exile—with Larisa Bogoraz-Daniel, the
wife of the writer—for publicly protesting the Soviet invasion of
Czechoslovakia.

Petitions denouncing these trials and comparing them to the
"shameful trials of the thirties" came to the Soviet leaders signed by
many artists, including Konstantin Paustovsky.

There was, indeed, a wave of trials of artists and intellectuals.
During January 1966, the time of the Sinyavsky-Daniel trial, more
than two hundred university professors, students, journalists, writers,
and scientists were secretly tried in Kiev for having distributed
pamphlets in defense of Ukrainian culture and urging the use of
the Ukrainian language in the Ukrainian Republic. Citations of the
freedoms of speech, press, and assembly guaranteed by the Soviet
constitution were of no help to the defendants.

In Leningrad, a year later, several hundred persons were arrested,
including university professors and students, poets, literary critics
and magazine editors. They were charged with conspiracy to commit armed rebellion. One of those arrested, the editor of a multi-
volume work on Dostoevsky, was sentenced to thirteen years at hard
labor.

As if to compensate for its restraint in no longer exacting the death
penalty for political dissidence, the Soviet government has supple-
mented the usual punishments of exile and imprisonment with that
of the commitment of certain defendants to mental institutions.

Among the artists forced to live among the insane were Valery Tarsis, the author of several anti-Soviet stories published abroad, among them "Ward 7," a description of his stay in a mental hospital, styled after "Ward 6," a Chekhov story about an insane asylum; A. Yesenin-Volpin, a poet and son of the poet Sergei Yesenin; M. Naritsa-Narymov, a sculptress who published a poetic protest abroad; and N. Gorbanevskaya, a poetess who publicly protested the Soviet Union's invasion of Czechoslovakia.

The most outspoken and persistent critic of this repression has been Alexander Solzhenitsyn, the novelist, who wrote of one victim: "It is precisely for the diversity of his gifts that he has been charged with abnormality; a split personality. It is precisely his sensitivity to injustice, to stupidity, that is made to seem a sick deviation; poor adaptation to the social milieu. Once you don't think as you are ordered to think, you are abnormal! And well-adapted people—they must all think alike."

Further, he added, "There is no restraint of law. Even the appeals of our best scientists and writers are bounced back like peas off a wall.

"If only this were the first case! But it has become a fashion, a devious method of reprisal without searching for a fault, when the real cause is too shameful to be stated . . .

"They said he had concern for social problems, excess ardor and excessive sang-froid, too brilliant abilities and lack of them.

"But even simple common sense should act as a restraint. Remember that Chadayev in his time was not even touched. . . . It is short-sighted to think that you can live, constantly relying on force alone, constantly scorning the objections of conscience."[56]

Thus, in the years since Stalin's death, Soviet cultural life has traveled almost full circle, from purge to thaw and back to repression. For a time the fortunes of the artists soared to new latitudes of freedom. But when this only generated demands for more freedom, the reaction set in. The iconography of Stalin himself told the story. When his pictures disappeared, the climate for artists was friendly and warm. In recent years as his picture reappeared in movies,

56. *New York Times,* June 17, 1970.

books, and exhibits, and his bust appeared at his grave at the Kremlin wall, repression reigned again. Significantly, that bust was carved
personally by the president of the Academy of Arts, Nikolai V.
Tomsky.

Control: How It's Done

Art in Russia today is big business, state business. It probably
represents the largest governmental enterprise in culture and cre-
ativity in the world, bountifully supported with the economic resources of a giant nation and energetically restrained by the political
powers of a huge totalitarian system.

The Soviet government was quick to recognize the political, technical, and educational advantages of art. Tickets for movies, concerts, and the theater are inexpensive. Admission to museums and
art shows is easily afforded by the average citizen. Talented children
and interested adults can usually gain access to free or inexpensive
lessons in music, art, dance, and drama.

About five hundred professional companies of actors, dancers, and
musicians perform before a hundred million people each year. The
major productions are in the largest cities, but even remote regions
have been given the means of establishing resident companies of
performers. Books, too, are relatively inexpensive and the government supports four hundred thousand libraries throughout the country.

Young people aspiring to a career in the arts can obtain instruction
in school or in the Communist party's youth-club houses. In certain
high schools students may concentrate on the arts while also getting
a general education. Those who pass special examinations move on
to tuition-free four- and five-year institutes. After this training they
usually have little difficulty gaining admission to the professional
unions of artists. Technically their education is thought to be of a
high level, especially in the theater arts.

Most professional artists live the equivalent of a middle-class Soviet life, but the most successful can achieve a truly enviable position.
Internationally famous performers like David Oistrakh, the violinist,
and Mstislav Rostropovich, the cellist, earn such large fees abroad

The Moiseyev Folk Dance Ensemble. *Sovfoto*

for the government that employs them that they are allowed to import foreign goods at will and also to draw, without limit, on open-ended bank accounts in the Soviet Union.

Igor Moiseyev, the Bolshoi Theater choreographer and leader of the Moiseyev Folk Dance troupe, maintains several residences in the Soviet Union, including a luxury apartment in Moscow and a country house near the Black Sea. Rostropovich can afford to indulge his enthusiasm for antiques and is probably one of the few Soviet citizens who has the physical space to house and enjoy them. Mikhail Sholokhov, the Nobel prize winner, has a small plane at his disposal. Automobiles, which are extremely difficult to obtain by the average citizen, come easily to the prominent artists and performers.

Slightly less distinguished artists, however, live in much more modest circumstances. Often artists will band together and build a cooperative apartment house, in which every member of a particular theater or of a local union is given living space.

Membership in one of the artists' unions includes the opportunity to work and rest in seclusion at writers' and artists' colonies scattered throughout the country, to enjoy paid vacations at spas on the Black Sea, and to qualify for trips abroad. Soviet citizens are not free to travel, even if they have the money, without special permission from the government. Most who get that permission must travel in groups, always accompanied by secret police agents and informers.

Membership in the unions is not automatic; it depends as much on conformity and political orthodoxy as on artistic talent.

The standard of acceptability was made clear in the trial of the poet, Yosef Brodsky, in 1964. Brodsky was accused of being a parasite, the Soviet government's definition of a person who is not working at an approved occupation in the approved manner. Since Brodsky's poetry did not conform to party-line standards, he was not a member of the writers' union. In turn, he was accused of not working, of being a parasite. His interrogation by the judge reveals these different definitions of work:

Judge: What is your profession?

Brodsky: A lyric poet. A translator.

Judge: Who has recognized you as a poet? Who has determined that you belong to the category of poets?

Brodsky: Nobody. Who determined that I am in the category of human beings?

Judge: Have you studied this?

Brodsky: What?

Judge: To be a poet. You have not made any efforts to obtain an institutional—a higher—education, to study. . . .

Brodsky: I don't think it's possible to study to be a poet.

Judge: Why not?

Brodsky: That's from God. . . .

Judge: What can you say about the degree of your participation in our great movement forward toward communism?

Brodsky: The building of communism doesn't mean just working at a lathe or plowing a field. It means mental work too.

Judge: In our country everyone is obliged to work. How have you been able to remain idle so long?

Brodsky: Then you don't consider my work to be work . . .[57]

Union members are expected to create poems, paintings, and compositions for special state occasions, such as May Day, or November 7, the anniversary of the 1917 revolution. The cooperating artist, in turn, can expect handsome fees and commissions from farms and factories. The unions also arrange for the exhibition and publication of his work and appoint him to the editorial boards of publishing houses and magazines.

Behind the unions, whose politically attuned leaders are really the agents of the Central Committee of the Communist Party, stands the power and the purse of the party and government.

The government adds to the privileges and rewards of the better artists. It distributes titles of honor, as the czars once did and the British monarch still does—"Merited Worker of the Arts," "Merited Artist," and "People's Artist"—either of a single republic or of the entire country, in ascending order of importance. These honors bring money, status, and further privilege.

The government also distributes prizes, the most coveted of which are named for Lenin (formerly for Stalin). They carry a cash value of more than $10,000 each and bring a flood of laudatory publicity. As the poet Yevtushenko has written of the days of scarcity under Stalin, the prizes also meant "appointment to some official post, a car, an apartment—without being on the waiting list—and possibly even a summer house. Many writers and poets didn't give a damn whether anybody read the book that got them the prize. What they cared about was the prize."[58]

Still, an artistic career in the Soviet Union can be a mixed blessing. In return for state training, artists and performers are expected to fill positions in outlying regions; only the very best and luckiest ever reach fame in the big cities. Moreover, failure to get along with the leaders of the art unions can result in severe economic sanctions. Above all, the government, party, and unions demand observance of the political and stylistic limits decreed for all the arts. The artists who do not respond to these orders and inducements are quickly restrained in their work by political censorship and economic sanc-

57. Yuri Krotkov, *I am From Moscow: A View of the Russian Miracle* (New York: E. P. Dutton, 1967), p. 207.
58. Yevtushenko, *A Precocious Autobiography,* p. 77.

tions, followed by actual arrest, prison, ostracism, and exile. Because the best artists are always straining at this leash, they live their lives in constant contest with the party censor.

The official censorship of writings follows a set routine: all books and magazines must be cleared for publication by a government censor. He may demand changes in the work and, when it suits him, may delay publication indefinitely, even of a magazine whose subscriptions are already paid. Most books are given trial runs in the literary magazines. In this way the censor often gets a second chance at a work after he has measured its political and critical reception.

Even publication between hard covers does not secure a book against censorship. Ilya Ehrenburg recalls that during the 1937 purges one of his books was circulated with one page much shorter and whiter than the rest; it was reprinted and pasted in at the last moment to delete the names of men recently convicted of crimes against the state.

This cut-and-paste routine is sometimes openly confessed. The owners of the Great Soviet Encyclopedia receive orders from time to time to cut out a few pages and substitute new ones, so as to eliminate some fallen figure from history or to inscribe a new historical "truth." Eliminating their own former idols from history has become a special talent of censors. In a movie about the Communist party's twentieth congress in 1956, at which Khrushchev denounced Stalin, the event was portrayed without once picturing or mentioning either man.

The censorship can be suffocating, but it is often merely capricious. As one writer pointed out in 1968, "In Leningrad, the play *Dion* was prohibited; in Moscow it was authorized. The film *Before the Tribunal of History* was authorized in Moscow and Leningrad, but it was prohibited in Gorky and some other cities and towns. One of the Moscow literary reviews was forbidden to mention the name of Solzhenitsyn, even in an article devoted to Soviet literature abroad. But an editorial office on a neighboring street was permitted to do so."

Theater companies do not know how they will fare with the censor until they have completed production of a performance. Their censors, called instructors and inspectors, watch the final rehearsals and only then order changes or prohibit the show from opening. Occasionally, a show is cancelled even after opening night and the public sale of tickets.

Because the censorship is primarily political, the chief politician often ends up being the principal censor. The more difficult a decision, the higher it is passed. Former Premier Khrushchev is known to have personally authorized the publication of Solzhenitsyn's account of life in a labor camp, *One Day in the Life of Ivan Denisovich*, and Yevtushenko's poem, "Stalin's Heirs." When conservative painters wanted to close an exhibition of young abstractionists, they took Khrushchev to the hall and made certain that everyone heard his harangue against the art that he could not comprehend.

And because they are political, the standards of the censors are constantly changing. Khrushchev approved the book about labor camps in 1962 because it accorded with his then lively campaign against the terrors of Stalinism. But when he found his countrymen eager to rake up the past and overturn it altogether while foreigners gloated over these exposures of the horrors of Soviet life, he suddenly banned all further prison memoirs.

Normally, there is trouble with the censor whenever a work reflects badly on an aspect of Soviet life or politics. Censorship is carried out in the name of protecting the country from the criticism of foreign enemies, but it is doubtful that such work would win official favor even if there were no enemies or foreigners.

Because the party's preferences and complaints change constantly, the most pernicious censorship is probably done by the artists themselves. Alexander Tvardovsky (1910–1971), a famous poet and for many years the editor of *Novy Mir*, once examined this phenomenon in a poem called "Vista Beyond Vista." He described a trip to Siberia during which fellow passengers openly criticize contemporary literature and draw the poet into equally candid responses. Another passenger, whom Tvardovsky represents as his "editor," is entertained by the bold talk of the poet and discovers that Tvardovsky had long suppressed his best thoughts. This editor was a very special kind, he said, created inside the poet by the fear of himself. "You are doing all my work for me," the editor concluded.[59]

Anatoly Kuznetsov, a writer who defected to England in 1969,

59. Alexandrova, *op. cit.*, p. 341.

has said that each of his novels exists in three versions: one for himself, a second with the truth "lacquered" over so that it would please the editors and the censors, and the third "banal" version which, after more cuts, deletions and rewritings, finally reached the reader.

When all the inducements and restraints fail to work, there is the final punishment—and reward—of the police. The Soviet secret police is not content to watch over writers and manage their arrest and prosecution when the party demands. It also seeks to enlist some of them, perhaps all, to spy and inform upon the others, often at home and always abroad. When Kuznetsov finally decided to leave his family and home to seek a new career in the West, he could not get permission to travel out of the country until he had taken to the police a false story accusing Yevtushenko and others of plotting to publish a new underground magazine. Mysteriously, he added, "Perhaps Yevtushenko will one day tell of the conditions on which he was allowed to travel round the world and the reports he had to write."[60]

Kuznetsov's defection from the Soviet Union aroused not only the anger of the secret police, but also the scorn of his fellow writers, such as Andrei Almarik. Almarik later wrote, "What, in effect, threatened the Russian writer [Kuznetsov] if, before his first visit abroad, he had refused to collaborate with the KGB [secret police]? The writer would not have gone abroad, but he would have remained an honest man. In refusing to collaborate he would have lost a part, perhaps a considerable part, of his external freedom, but he would have achieved greater inner freedom."[61]

Almarik's remark points to the heart of the nonconformist writer's dilemma in the Soviet Union: if he wishes to remain true to himself, he will probably not be published; if he cannot publish, he will find it very difficult to survive as a writer. If he defects, he will be free to write as he wishes, but once out of his homeland, will he still be inspired to create?

The only uncensored artistic work in the Soviet Union today is the considerable amount produced surreptitiously for friends or self. Nonconforming writers, painters, sculptors, and composers often create to government order by day, but in a wholly different style

60. London *Daily Telegraph*, as reprinted in the *New York Times*, August 10, 1969.
61. Andrei Almarik, *Will the Soviet Union Survive until 1984?* (New York: Harper & Row, and the Alexander Herzen Foundation, 1970), pp. ix–x.

at night. Some of their work is secreted away for another day. Some is reproduced by private means and circulated illegally. And some is smuggled out of the country, with hopes of foreign dissemination.

Readers and audiences exist for the underground creators in growing numbers because public enthusiasm and support is the one thing the party cannot decree. It can get writers to write what it wants, but it cannot make readers read or even buy. Approved histories and novels languish on the shelves of state stores and libraries, and to this day Soviet consumers prefer Russian classics to most of the approved art of the post-revolutionary period.

The Soviet art system is pervasive and it is, in many respects, impressive in size and scope. But whatever it achieves in the mass is compromised by the pain and tyranny it imposes on its most creative minds. Today's condemnation of the system by Alexander Solzhenitsyn, one of the most eminent and popular Soviet writers, bears a striking resemblance to that uttered fifty years ago, at the very beginning of the Communist period, by the equally eminent writer, Yevgeni Zamyatin.

"I am afraid that we shall have no real literature as long as Russia's citizenry is looked upon as a child whose innocence must be protected," Zamyatin wrote in 1921. "I am afraid that we shall have no real literature until we cure ourselves of a certain new Catholicism which fears every word of heresy in no lesser degree than the old."[62]

"Literature cannot develop in between the categories of 'permitted' and 'not permitted,' 'about this you may write' and 'about this you may not,' " wrote Solzhenitsyn in 1967. "Literature that is not the breath of contemporary society, that dares not transmit the pains and fears of that society, that does not warn in time against threatening moral and social dangers—such literature does not deserve the name of literature; it is only a facade. Such literature loses the confidence of its own people, and its published works are used as waste paper instead of being read."[63]

Unable to publish and withstand the social and economic pressures, Zamyatin wrote a letter to Stalin in 1931 asking permission to emigrate: "The death of my tragedy *Attila* was a genuine tragedy for me. It made entirely clear to me the futility of any effort at chang-

---

62. *Problems of Communism*, November/December 1964, p. 31.
63. *Ibid.*, September/October 1968, p. 38.

ing my situation, especially in view of the well-known affair involving my novel *We*, which followed soon after. . . . The manhunt organized at the time was unprecedented in Soviet literature, and was remarked on even in the foreign press. I became an object of fear to my erstwhile friends, publishers, and theaters. My books were banned from the libraries. My play (*The Flea*), presented with unvarying success by the Second Moscow Art Theater for four seasons, was withdrawn from the repertory. The publication of my collected works by the Federation Publishing House was halted. Any publishing organization that attempted to publish my works was immediately placed under fire."[64]

Unable to publish and unable to any longer withstand the pressure on him, Solzhenitsyn wrote a similar letter to the Union of Soviet Writers in 1967. He complained that his manuscript for *The First Circle* had been seized by the state security organizations; that his novel *The Cancer Ward* had been rejected for publication by numerous magazines; that a play, accepted by a theater, had not been approved for performance; and that a screenplay and other stories could find no outlet.

His letter, supported by a hundred other writers, proposed the "abolition of all censorship, open or hidden, of all fictional writing, which would release publishing houses from the obligation to obtain authorization for the publication of every printed page."[65]

Like Zamyatin, Solzhenitsyn appears now to live only as forbidden fruit, a tragic figure, but an inspiring one for younger writers because in spite of everything he still speaks out for the creative spirit of Russia.

As he wrote to the 1967 congress of Soviet writers: "Many writers have been subjected during their lifetime to abuse and slander in the press and from rostrums without being afforded the physical possibility of replying. More than that, they have been exposed to violence and personal persecution (Bolgakov, Akhmatova, Tsvetaeva, Pasternak, Zoshchenko, Platonov, Aleksandr Grin, Vasily Grossman). The Union of Writers not only did not make its own publications available to these writers for purposes of reply and justification, not only did not come out in their defense but *through*

64. Alexandrova, *op. cit.*, p. 108.
65. *Problems of Communism*, September/October 1968, p. 38.

its leadership was always first among the persecutors [italics added].
Names that adorned our poetry of the twentieth century found themselves on the list of those expelled from the union or not even admitted to it in the first place. The leadership of the union cravenly
abandoned to their distress those for whom persecution ended in
exile, labor camps, and death (Pavel Vasilev, Mandelstam, Artem
Vesely, Pilniak, Babel, Tabidze, Zabolotsky, and others). The list
must be cut off at 'and others.' We learned after the twentieth party
congress that there were more than six hundred writers whom the
union had obediently handed over to their fate in prisons and
camps."[66]

66. *Ibid.,* p. 38.

5. Conclusion: The Lost Trail of a Millennium

EVEN a brief glance at a thousand years of Russian cultural history reveals a great tradition of artistic expression and, in spite of despotic government restrictions—perhaps because of them —an eventual surge of great art.

It is a tradition that built up to a climax in the nineteenth and early twentieth centuries, when Russian writers and composers moved and dazzled their countrymen with a truly national voice that came to be heard throughout the world. They produced an unmistakable Russian literature, brooding like the Russian land mass, full of psychological and religious reflections and tensions and a mournful, romantic music. And then, riding the waves of revolution, there followed other writers and composers and painters and directors who blazed new paths of art and self-expression and infected artists everywhere.

Through the centuries of czarist autocracy, through wars and revolutions, the Russian arts flourished until suddenly, in the new Communist era that they had helped to evoke, the nation's artists and intellectuals were smothered in a blanket of conformity. Suddenly they were cut off, not only from the rest of the world, but from their own inspiring past. A struggle persists, but they cannot yet be said to have recovered or regained their voices.

The Soviet period has produced some good writing and some good music, most of it composed, however, by artists educated before the Bolshevik revolution. The good that has been produced does not begin to match the quality of the work of artists who were driven into exile or to their deaths. The most popular works in the Soviet Union today remain the classics that were composed more than a century ago.

A younger generation of artists has managed to lift the suffocating blanket a bit, but the significance of its work is more political than cultural. The best of it is a literature and graphic art of protest and defiance, borrowing the forbidden Western styles and themes and not yet linked to the daring innovators who were silenced in the 1930s. Two generations of evolution have been lost to Russian art. With the creative artists thus retarded, the most conspicuous cultural achievements have been attained by the performers of music and dance—especially soloists on the piano and violin and in the classical ballet.

Still, over the centuries, there are patterns of continuity, especially in the relationship of the Russian artist to his government. The artist has always striven for creative freedom, and the government has always tried to restrain and control him. Whether sustained by claims of the divine rights of czars or of the omniscience of the Communist party, the Russian governments have sought to use the arts and, when opposed by them, they have persevered in remarkably consistent methods for buying or forcing the artist's collaboration: censorship, exile, and even declarations of insanity.

Nonetheless, there were important differences. The czars did not try to impose a central doctrine on the artists. They were grateful enough for flattering portraits of themselves in words, stone, or song, for entertainment and education and the very production of something that the world could recognize as culture. Critics in the czarist years were able to reach independent judgments and often became the inspiration of entire trends in Russian art.

The Soviet prescription for artists has been much more purposeful. It requires them to propagate Communist doctrine in a "socialist realist" manner and to manipulate public opinion, aspirations, and taste. The critic has been turned into a political supervisor of the arts, and cultural contact with the rest of the world has been permitted only in small and carefully supervised doses.

Throughout Russian and Soviet history, however, the nation's art has faced aesthetically westward. Although Russia has been physically and politically sealed for long periods, and although it covers much more territory in Asia than in Europe and has absorbed millions of people from hundreds of different ethnic groups, its cultural inspirations over the centuries have come from the West, and the most creative of its artists have addressed themselves to the peoples of the West.

But Russian artists have also been remarkably loyal to their homeland. They have usually felt bound to the Russian environment and have longed for it even in exile. The youngest artists in Russia today know that they have a rich cultural heritage and they seek to move forward by retracing their nation's steps, by discovering lost traditions, and the promise of greatness. They are agitating to have the still-censored work of their grandfathers retrieved from museum storerooms, printed once again in books, and revived in concert halls and theaters.

Essentially, their campaign is aimed at creative freedom, but it has evolved into a broader movement in reaction to the government's repressive methods. Feeling deprived and aroused, Russian intellectuals have joined again with the artists to protect their tormentors and to enlarge their opportunities. The art that was born in religious orthodoxy a millennium ago is now engaged in a battle of liberation for political as well as creative freedom.

BIBLIOGRAPHY

General History

Pares, Bernard. *A History of Russia*. New York: Alfred A. Knopf, 1953. Emphasis on the pre-revolutionary period.

Culture

Billington, James. *The Icon and the Axe*. New York: Alfred A. Knopf, 1966. A survey of the Russian cultural and intellectual scene.

Horizon Book of the Arts of Russia. New York: American Heritage Publishing Company, 1970. Includes many color photographs and literary excerpts.

Johnson, Priscilla. *Khrushchev and the Arts. The Politics of Soviet Culture, 1962–1964*. Cambridge, Mass.: The M.I.T. Press, 1965. Contains documents of a short but significant period in Soviet cultural history.

Miliukov, Paul. *Outlines of Russian Culture*. Edited by Michael Karpovich. Philadelphia: University of Pennsylvania Press, 1948. Essays on literature, art, architecture and music. Emphasis is on the pre-revolutionary period.

Art and Architecture

Gray, Camilla. *The Great Experiment—Russian Art 1863–1922*. New York: Harry Abrams, 1962. Many color plates.

Hamilton, George Heard. *The Art and Architecture of Russia*. Harmondsworth, Middlesex: Penguin Books, Ltd., 1954. Includes 180 pages of pictures. On pre-revolutionary Russia.

Kornilovich, Kira. *Arts of Russia. Origins to End of Sixteenth Century*. Cleveland: World Publishing Company, 1967.

Koslow, Jules. *The Kremlin—Eight Centuries of Tyranny and Terror*. New York: Thomas Nelson and Son, 1958.

Rice, Tamara Talbot. *A Concise History of Russian Art*. New York: Frederick A. Praeger, 1963. (Paperback) Pre-revolutionary period only.

Voyce, Arthur. *The Moscow Kremlin*. Berkeley and Los Angeles: University of California Press, 1954.

Ballet

Fokine, Mikhail. *Fokine. Memoirs of a Ballet Master*. Translated by Vitale Fokine. Edited by Anatole Chujoy. Boston: Little, Brown and Company, 1961.

187

Karsavina, Tamara. *Theater Street.* New York: E. P. Dutton and Company, 1931, 1950. An autobiography by a prominent Russian ballerina.

Lifar, Serge. *A History of Russian Ballet from its Origin to the Present Day.* London: Hutchinson, 1954.

Decorative Arts

Bainbridge, Henry Charles. *Peter Carl Fabergé—His Life and Work.* London: B. T. Batsford, Ltd., 1949.

Ovsyannikov, Y. *Russian Folk Arts and Crafts.* Moscow: Progress Publishers.

Literature: History

Alexandrova, Vera. *A History of Soviet Literature: 1917–1964. From Gorky to Solzhenitsyn.* Garden City, New York: Doubleday, 1963. (Paperback). Includes a bibliography of Russian literature available in translation.

Carlisle, Olga Andreyev. *Voices in the Snow.* New York: Random House, 1962. Interviews with Soviet authors of the early 1960s.

Mirsky, D. S. *A History of Russian Literature.* New York: Alfred A. Knopf, 1949. Emphasis on the pre-revolutionary period.

Slonim, Marc. *The Epic of Russian Literature. From its Origins Through Tolstoy.* New York: Oxford University Press, 1964. (Paperback)

———. *From Chekhov to the Revolution: Russian Literature 1900–1917.* New York: Oxford University Press, 1962. (Paperback)

———. *Soviet Russian Literature: Writers and Problems 1917–1967.* New York: Oxford University Press, 1967. (Paperback)

Literature: Biography

Simmons, Ernest J. *Chekhov, A Biography.* Boston: Little, Brown and Company, 1962.

———. *Leo Tolstoy:* Volume I, *The Years of Development 1828–1879;* Volume II, *The Years of Maturity, 1880–1910.* New York: Vintage Books, 1960. (Paperback)

Troyat, Henri. *Tolstoy.* Garden City, New York: Doubleday, 1967.

Literature: Original works in anthologies

Blake, Patricia, and Heyward, Max, editors. *Halfway to the Moon. New Writing from Russia.* Garden City, New York: Doubleday, 1965. (Paperback)

Guerney, Bernard Guilbert. *An Anthology of Russian Literature in the Soviet Period from Gorki to Pasternak.* New York: Random House, 1960. (Paperback). Writers who made their literary reputations in the 1920s and 1930s.

Kamen, Isai. *Great Russian Stories.* New York: Random House, 1959. (Paperback) From Pushkin through Bunin.

McLean, Hugh, and Vickery, Walter N., translators and editors. *The Year of Protest, 1956. An Anthology of Soviet Literary Materials.* New York: Vintage Books, 1961. (Paperback)

Noyes, George Rapall, editor. *Masterpieces of the Russian Drama*, 2 vols. New York: Dover Publications, 1960. (Paperback). Pre-revolutionary period.

Reeve, F. D., editor. *Great Soviet Short Stories.* New York: Dell Publishing Company, 1962. (Paperback)

Zenkovsky, Serge A. *Medieval Russia's Epics, Chronicles and Tales.* New York: E. P. Dutton and Company, 1963. (Paperback)

Music

Calvocaressi, M. D., and Abraham, Gerald. *Masters of Russian Music.* New York: Alfred A. Knopf, 1936. Biographies of nineteenth-century composers.

Olkhovsky, Andrey. *Music Under the Soviets.* New York: Praeger, 1955.

Theater and Cinema

Gorchakov, Nikolai. *The Theater in Soviet Russia.* Translated by Edgar Lehrman. New York: Columbia University Press, 1957. The first thirty years of the Soviet theater.

Houghton, Norris. *Return Engagement.* New York: Holt, Rinehart and Winston, 1962. An American theatrical producer revisits the Soviet Union after twenty-five years.

Leyda, Jay. *Kino: A History of Russian and Soviet Film.* New York: Macmillan, 1966.

Slonim, Marc. *Russian Theater. From the Empire to the Soviets.* New York: Collier Books, 1962. (Paperback) Includes discussion of ballet, cinema and opera.

Stanislavsky, Konstantin. *My Life in Art.* Moscow: Foreign Languages Publishing House. Translated by G. Ivanov-Mumjiev.

Readers particularly interested in the Soviet period should consult *Problems of Communism*, United States Information Agency, Washington, D. C., a scholarly bimonthly journal. Soviet materials in Russian and English can be obtained from Four Continents Book Corporation, 156 Fifth Avenue, New York, New York; Kamkin's Russian Bookstore, 12224 Parklawn Drive, Rockville, Maryland; or Znanie Bookstore, 5237 Geary Blvd., San Francisco, California, 94118.

Index